CURIOUS AND HUMOROUS CUSTOMS

CURIOUS
AND HUMOROUS
CUSTOMS

compiled by

DON LEWIS

MOWBRAYS

LONDON & OXFORD

© A. R. Mowbray & Co. Ltd. 1972

Printed in Great Britain by
Alden & Mowbray Ltd at the Alden Press, Oxford

ISBN 0 264 64584 7

First published 1972
by A. R. Mowbray & Co. Ltd
The Alden Press, Osney Mead
Oxford, OX2 0EG

ACKNOWLEDGEMENTS

The compiler would like to offer his very real thanks to all those who have contributed to the making of this book.

To all the clergy who have generously shared their knowledge, particularly the Right Reverend Eric Gordon, Archdeacon D. E. M. Glynne Jones, the Reverend Canon M. Ridgway, FSA, author of *The Cheshire Goldsmiths* for permission to browse in his library, the Reverend Canon J. R. Alford, and the Reverend J. C. Sladden.

To Richard Mulkern, his publisher, Don Lewis owes more than usual thanks for extraordinary solicitude: prompting, superhuman patience, and good humour.

Amongst the laity, he is indebted to the members of the Carmarthenshire Antiquarian Society for an exciting day visiting holy wells, to Dick Morgan, Esquire, of the Dolau Angling Club, Stanley Bailey, Esquire, and Walter Pryce, Esquire, both of Castle Caereinion; to Mrs Mary Jones for access to the manuscripts and books of the late J. C. Jones, Bishop of Bangor, and in special measure to J. D. K. Lloyd, Esquire, of Montgomery, for infecting him with his own love for the things of antiquity.

As always, the compiler's debt to Mrs F. M. Williams, FLA, is quite incalculable. She and her staff at the Library, Hale, Cheshire, have never flagged in their efforts to obtain obscure books for research, nor has their good humour ever failed.

The great pillars of the past also deserve acknowledgement: S. Baring-Gould, P. H. Ditchfield, R. S. Hawker,

Dean Spence, Mackenzie Walcott, Abbot Gasquet, William Andrews, J. E. Vaux, J. Christie, William Henderson, S. H. Edwards, Dean Hook, T. F. Thistleton-Dyer, Richard Polwhele, F. J. Snell, J. S. Burn, A. M. Burke, R. E. Chester.

And more recently, acknowledgement is made, with sincere thanks, to the following for permission to use copyright material: to Penguin Books Ltd for the extract from Geoffrey Chaucer: *The Canterbury Tales* (*The Prologue*) translated by Nevill Coghill, Copyright(©) Nevill Coghill, 1951, 1958, 1960; to Professor David Knowles and the Cambridge University Press for extracts from *Religious Orders in England*; to Miss Dora Robertson for the extract from her book, *Sarum Close* published by Forecrest Publishing Ltd, Bath; and to the Society for Promoting Christian Knowledge for a short extract from *The Monks Of Chester* by R. V. H. Burne.

In such a book as *Curious and Humorous Customs* there are, unfortunately, bound to be some omissions of acknowledgement of copyright. These are, of course, lamentable, and should there be any such oversights in this work, the compiler offers his unqualified apologies.

Last and lastingly, Don Lewis makes mention of his wife and ghost.

FOR

Stanley Bailey, Esquire,
Parish Clerk of Castle

and

Edwin Combs, Esquire,
Verger of Hale St Peter

CONTENTS

INTRODUCTION

'I don't know what people nowadays would do for customs if it weren't for the likes of us in old country places', Stan Bailey, parish clerk of Castle would say. 'We got our roots deep down in the ground, not tottering on a few bricks like what folks in these new concrete cities have. You'll only find real customs born and bred out of Time and the Soil.'

Some of the customs familiar to our forefathers have remained to this day: like the giving to the bridegroom of one of the bride's old shoes by her father as a token of the transference of authority; or that of showering the young bridal couple with confetti—a custom widely observed nowadays yet not so generally understood. Many old customs have, however, not survived, and it is with the hope of preserving some of them that the compiler has recorded those found in this book.

Inevitably, the selection chosen will reflect the interest and bias of that compiler, but the general source of it is common to all, and consequently of interest to anyone with a feel for and a love of the traditions which nourished our ancestors through the various milestones of life.

It is, in the main, a light-hearted collection, intended to afford those unfortunates now removed from the glorious rural scene a mirthful and interesting share of the rich heritage of manners and customs of their forefathers, and it is as such that it is now humbly offered.

January 1972   D.L.

I

Birth Controlled

ONE-ARMED CHRISTIANS

In sixteenth-century Ireland there was an odd but severely practical custom that in baptism the right arms of male children were left untouched by holy water so that they might be free to deal underhand and therefore more deadly blows in battle. It must be remembered that baptism at that time was by total immersion in the font.

CHEESE ASSISTED DELIVERY

As soon as a child was born in the old days, it was the custom to pass the child through the ring of the rind of a cheese. It was more than likely that a piece of the cheese from which the rind had been taken had been given to the mother prior to the birth of the child in order to speed up the delivery.

KEEP THE HAGS AWAY

All sorts of charms were employed to protect the newly born child from harm. Charms like rosemary, a knife, a bar of iron, a piece of silver, were sometimes put in the cradle with the baby. A very old custom was to place under the baby's head a piece of bread blessed by a priest. Herrick, in his Hesperides, says this:

Bring the Holy crust of bread,
Lay it underneath the head;
'Tis a certain charm to keep
Hags away while children sleep.

THE FIRST STEP

It was a custom that the first journey the new-born baby made should be upwards, therefore the midwife, or the woman attending the mother, would carry the baby upstairs; or if there were no staircase they would step up one or two rungs of a ladder. If there was no ladder available, they would even go to the length of standing with the baby on a stool. In the church this custom was observed by the raising of the font on steps.

FEARS FOR THE UNBAPTISED

A BELIEF prevailed that children, if they died unchristened, joined the ranks of the fairies or that their souls wandered about in the air restless and unhappy until the day of judgement. There was an interesting Northumberland custom of burying any unbaptised child at the feet of an adult Christian corpse for protection.

AVOID UNWANTED HAIR

IT used to be the custom that any boys presented for baptism had to be christened before any girl candidates. It was thought that if the girls were baptised before the boys they would have hair on their faces when they grew up.

GOOD CASE FOR 'LADIES FIRST'

THE idea of having a child baptised in a new church was terrifying to parents. The Revd S. Baring-Gould recorded that in Yorkshire there was even a strong objection to having a child baptised in a new font.

Said a parson to a parent of a child requiring baptism— 'Why not have your child baptised in the new font?'

'Nay,' he said, 'if t'were a lass I shouldn't mind, but as it's a lad I'll not risk it.'

The idea was that the first child baptised in a font would most surely die.

CRY THE DEVIL AWAY

MOTHERS will often say that their children don't 'do well' until they are baptised. There is a superstition that the child ought to cry at baptism and indeed in some parts of the country the parish priest makes the child cry by giving it a pinch. It appears that the crying signifies the expulsion of the evil spirit.

WATER BABIES

A BARBAROUS custom is recorded in Burt's 'Letters from a Gentleman in the North of Scotland to his Friend in London' published in 1754 (*Gentleman's Magazine*).

The moment a child is born it is plunged into cold water, though it should be necessary first to break the ice. At the christening, the father holds it up before the pulpit, and receives a long extemporary admonition concerning its education.

FIRE INSURANCE

YET another custom which existed in olden days was 'Baptism by Fire'. After the child was brought home from the christening service, it was held for a few moments over the fire while the sentence was intoned, 'Let the flame consume thee now or never.' This was supposed to be an omen for good to protect the child from death by fire as it grew up. Death by burning, was of course, quite common in primitive villages where fire was a constant hazard.

A ROBE OF INNOCENCE

THE chrisom was a white cloth put on the head of a child at baptism. After the immersion in water, the priest made the sign of the cross on the child's head with oil, then the chrisom was put on, the priest asking at the same time the child's name and saying:

> Receive this white, pure and holy vestment which thou shalt wear before the tribunal of our Lord Jesus Christ that thou mayest inherit eternal life. Amen

It was to be worn for seven days. After the Reformation, the use of oil was omitted, and the chrisom was worn by the child until the mother was churched, when it was returned to the priest. If the child died before churching, it was buried in the chrisom. Baptised children who died within a month of their baptism, were generally shrouded in the white cloth 'chrisom' put on the child's head at baptism, and because of this they were termed 'chrisoms'. Babes dying in their innocence, even down to the end of the eighteenth century were called chrisoms even though the practice of chrisom was expunged from the Prayer Book of 1552.

> This day is mine and yours, but ye know not what shall be on the morrow; and every morning creeps out a dark cloud, leaving behind it an ignorance and silence, deep as midnight, and undiscerned as are the phantasms that make a chrisome child to smile.
>
> Bishop Taylor, *Holy Living*

BREAD AND CHEESE SHARING

IN the Isle of Man there was a custom that when the baby was taken to church for baptism the woman carrying the child took with her bread and cheese to give to the first man she met for the purpose of saving the child from witchcraft or the fairies. In Scotland an unmarried woman invariably carried the child to church. The bread and cheese was wrapped up, and fastened with a pin taken from the child's dress. The male she presented this to became the child's 'first-foot': if he were a dark-haired man there would be good luck for the child.

The story is recorded of a certain English duke who, when visiting Glasgow, was strolling along a street on a Sunday afternoon. A young woman came up to him with a child in her arms and offered him a piece of bread and cheese. In vain he protested that he had nothing to do with the child—that he was C. of E. and knew nothing of the customs of the Presbyterian Kirk, and that she should leave him alone. The young woman continued to hold out authoritatively the bread and cheese. He used his last line of defence. 'Do you know, young lady, that I am the Duke of ——?'

Her reply was forceful: 'Though ye were the King on the throne, sir, ye must tak' that bread an' cheese.'

OLD WELSH CUSTOM

A NON-PAROCHIAL register recorded the baptism of Margaret and Jane David at Llangwebach, Glamorganshire:

Those were Twins, their mother died at their birth and the children were baptised at her funeral on their mother's coffin.

SPOONING TO SPOONS IN NINE MONTHS

CUPS and spoons, usually of silver, were presented to the newly baptised child. About four hundred years ago such spoons took on a special pattern and were called 'Apostle' spoons because the handle was moulded in the shape of one of the Apostles. This again was a protective token. It may be that the saying, 'He was born with a silver spoon in his mouth', owed its origin to this custom.

EARLY ROMAN PRACTICE

THE seventeenth-century custom was to give corals to a baby, and especially to a baby girl. Indeed, this practice is common even today. Its aim was to ward off the 'evil eye'. This, of course, was derived from Roman usage.

2

Shades of Eden

KEPT AT PIN'S LENGTH

'1667, 20th August. Turned into St Dunstan's church, where I heard an able sermon of the minister of the place; and stood by a pretty, modest maid, whom I did labour to take by the hand; but she would not, but got further and further from me; and at last I could perceive her to take pins out of her pocket to prick me if I should touch her again—which seeing, I did forbear, and was glad I did spy her design. And then I fell to gaze upon another pretty maid in a pew close to me, and she on me; and I did go about to take her by the hand, which she suffered a little, and then withdrew. So the sermon ended, and the church broke up, and my amours ended also.'

Pepys

SEGREGATION OF THE SEXES

THE custom of separating the sexes in church prevailed into the early part of the nineteenth century and is even now the practice in certain rural areas of North Wales. The men occupied one side of the nave and the women the other.

Some lines of doggerel summed up this old custom:

The churches and chapels we usually find
Are places where men unto women are joined;
But at Christ Church it seems they are more
    cruel-hearted,
For men and their wives are brought there to be parted.

The church referred to was Christ Church, Birmingham, where the rule of segregating the sexes in church was abolished in 1860.

On one occasion, the curate of Cottenham, in Cambridgeshire, stopped during his sermon, as someone was talking, and said, 'I heard a noise.'

The occupant of a seat on the women's side of the church said, 'Please sir, it is not us.'

Replied the curate, 'I'm glad to hear it, it will be the sooner over.'

BRING YOUR OWN PEW

ABOUT ninety years ago, the Revd Alfred N. Bull, of Woolavington, Bridgewater, wrote:

> I have officiated in churches where the separation of the sexes was very striking from all the men wearing the rustic costume of white smocks, and all the women red cloaks and black bonnets. The nave of my father's very large church at Saffron Waldon was always filled with red cloaks, the wearers each bringing a stool from the bottom of the church for her own use, and taking it back again after the service.

MIND WHERE YOU SIT

MANY curious customs are attached to pews. During the fifteenth century and much later in certain parishes, pews were reserved for men, for women and for young maidens. So we have from the records of the church of St Mary, Woolchurch, London, under 1541 and 1542:

> Paid for mending the mayden's pewe in the Church ijs.

In many churches there was a 'Churching pew'. This custom doubtless caused embarrassment to many ladies who were not aware of it. The story is told that an unmarried lady sat in the churching pew on one occasion. The Clerk came to her and asked, 'Have you a child to be christened, Ma'am?' whereupon the lady rushed home to her friend in a most embarrassed manner. 'My dear Charlotte! What has happened to you?' asked Mrs ——. 'Have you been robbed or insulted?' 'Worse, worse, much worse,' hysterically sobbed the old maid, 'I've been churched!'

A MALE CHURCHING

SIR THOMAS WIDDRINGTON, MP for York, in a speech in the House of Commons, told an extraordinary anecdote of a clergyman who was his friend and neighbour. A butcher in the parish was severely gored in the stomach by an ox, and only narrowly escaped death. Eventually, the wound being cured, the butcher desired to give public thanksgiving in the church for his safe deliverance. The puzzled clergyman, finding himself in a fix, anxious and willing to gratify his parishioner, and yet not knowing of any authorised form for such a public act, read the prayers for the churching of women.

Parliamentary History

CONFESS YOUR OWN SINS

IT is possible that the custom of the 'shriving-pew' ceased with the Reformation. This entailed the setting apart of a pew from which offenders did public penance.

T. F. Thiselton Dyer records one story which indicates this:

'These witnes in dede will not lye', as the poor man sayed by the priest, 'if I maybe homely to tell you a merry tale by the way'.

'A merry tale,' quoth I, 'commith never amyse to me.'

'The poor man,' quod he, 'had found ye priest over famyliar with his wife, and bycause he spake of it abrode and could not prouve it, the priest sued him before ye byshoppe's officiale for dyffamatyon, when the pore man upon paine of cursynge (i.e. excommunication), was commanded that in hys parishe churche, he should upon ye Sundaye, at high masse time, stande up and say, "mouth thy lyest". Whereupon for fulfilling of hys penance up was the pore soul set in a pew, that the people might wonder on hym and hyre what he sayd. And there all a lowed (when he had rehersyd what he had reported by the priest), then he sett hys handys on his mouthe, and said "Mouth! mouth, thou lyest!" and by-and-by, thereupon he set his hand upon his eyes, and said, "But eyen, eyen", quod he, "by ye Mass ye lye not a whitte!"'

SEXUAL ASSISTANCE AT A DAY OLD

In order that a child might grow up to find favour with the opposite sex, an article of the father's clothing used to be laid on the newly born female child, and a mother's petticoat on a male child.

ANOTHER USE FOR A ROLLING-PIN

Glass rolling-pins were regarded as charms to protect loved ones from the perils of the sea. They were given as presents full of perfume or spirits by sailors to their families and after their contents were used or consumed they were hung on the wall. Like love spoons these were very common in homes on the coastline of Wales and England.

GET A BLACK CAT, GIRLS

WHENEVER the cat o' the house is black
The lasses o' lovers will have no lack.

North Country rhyme

LET THE PUNISHMENT FIT THE CRIME

WHEN a woman had been convicted of brawling, or using abusive language, she was ordered by the magistrate to wear the 'brank' or 'scold's bridle'. A piece of iron in the contraption, which was locked around the woman's face and head, pressed down on the tongue. (This custom was

practised in Preston, in the House of Correction as recently
as 1854.)

COLD WATER CURE

THERE stands, my friend, in yonder pool,
An engine, called a Ducking-Stool;
By legal pow'r commanded down,
The joy, and terror of the town;
If jarring females kindle strife,
Give language foul, or lug the coif,
If noisy dames shou'd once begin,
To drive the house with horrid din,
Away, we cry, you'll grace the stool,
We'll teach you how your tongue to rule.
The fair offender fills the seat,
In sullen pomp profoundly great.

    And then,
Down in the deep the stool descends,
But here, at first, we miss our ends,
She mounts again, and rages more
Than ever vixen did before.

If so, my friend, pray let her take
A second turn into the lake,
And rather than your patience lose,
Thrice and again repeat the dose;
No brawling wives, no furious wenches,
No fire so hot, but water quenches.

Anon. *circa* 1720
(Contained in *Miscellaneous Poems*
by Benjamin West, 1780)

A CORRECTIVE RIDE

ANOTHER form of correction for naughty females was 'riding the stang'. An effigy of the offender was carried around the parish for exposure to public scorn, after which it was burnt in a public place while the onlookers hurled ridicule and missiles. This seems to have been used most often as a punishment for adultery. There was doubtless a time when the offender herself suffered the punishment, but over the years an effigy was substituted and the scorn and ridicule of neighbours for the person represented was considered to be adequate punishment.

ENCOURAGEMENT OF MATRIMONY AND HORSE RACING

IN the Parish of All Saints, Newmarket, in the early part of the nineteenth century, a marriage portion of £21 was given to any parishioner, who was, on Thursday in Easter week, married at the church to a woman belonging to it; neither party was to be under twenty or over twenty-five years of age, nor to be worth £20.

In the event of there being no claimants, the money, for that year only was to be paid to the winner of the race for the town plate.

CLERICAL CONCUBINE

DURING the sixteenth century the allure of the married state for the clergy in Wales was the cause of much complaint from stricter ecclesiastics. This complaint was recorded in the Warham Return which listed forty-three clergy in the diocese of Bangor charged with keeping 'concubines', that is, clergymen who had contracted uncanonical marriages, or marriages not recognised as such by the Western Church.

When Queen Mary came to the throne an attempt was made to deprive married clergy of their livings in order to bring back the Church to the obedience of the Church of Rome. On becoming Bishop of Bangor in 1555, William Glyn deprived many of the married clergy, but he generally gave them some other living in the diocese and often permitted them to exchange. This tolerance may have been due to the fact that he himself was one of a family of a married priest.

WASHING MOLLY GRIME

AN ancient custom in the parish of Glentham, Lincs, led to seven shillings being allotted annually to seven old maids as payment for their washing a tomb in Glentham church, called Molly Grime, with water brought from Newell Well.

'Molly Grime' was thus washed on every Good Friday and the old maids received their one shilling due.

BRUSH ASSISTED KNEELING

A CUSTOM associated with the Twelfth Night celebrations in the Yorkshire Dales was the Saturday night dance. The most interesting dance was the Elizabethan version of the snowball waltz. Men and women sat around the room and when the fiddlers got going a young man started the Whishin dance by picking up a cushion and placing it at the feet of the lady of his choice. They both knelt down and kissed, whereupon the lady picked up the cushion and placed it at the feet of the man she chose. This process went on until everyone in the room had a partner. The penalty for refusing to kneel took the form of gentle persuasion to the kneeling position with a brush. When the pairs were completed they went round the room singing:

> Arm in arm, round and round,
> Me that loves a bonny lass
> Will kiss her on the ground.

ADAM BY CRAB-APPLE

IN the West of England the village girls used to go up and down the hedges, gathering crab-apples, which they carried home. These they then laid out in the loft forming the initials of their prospective suitors' names. The initials which proved to be most perfect on old Michaelmas Day were considered to represent the strongest attachments and the best choice of husbands.

'FITNESS FOR MARRIAGE' TEST

LIFTING the heavy lid of a massive old chest housed in the parish church for keeping vestments and records, was quite often in olden times, the test for any young girl aiming to be a farmer's wife. These lids, with heavy iron clamps, like the one at Lower Peover, Cheshire, can barely be lifted with two hands. The old custom was that until the girl was fit enough to lift the lid with one hand, she was certainly not ready for the onerous duty of being a housewife.

SEX CHANGE RECORDED

'JAMES GODYKER of Barnston in the Parish of Wood-church, died in the year of our Lord 1525, left twenty marks to buy twenty yoke of Bullocks which were afterwards by order of the Commissioners of the Pious Uses, converted into cows given to the poor of the said Parish.'

Recorded in Woodchurch

HELPMEETS

WOMEN make men Love,
Love makes them sad,
Sadness makes them drink,
And drinking sets them mad.

WEEDING FOR CAKE AND KISSES

A SOMEWHAT quaint custom was that, at Eastertide, of corn-showing. The weed, cockle, which menaced the corn crop, was pulled out and the young man who did most work was allowed to claim a kiss from the maid of his choice at the celebration afterwards. He was also entitled to the largest piece of cake specially baked for the occasion.

'PIT-A-PAT, THE PAN'S HOT, I BE COME A-SHROVING'

THE housewives' race with pancakes in the village of Olney in Buckinghamshire was first run in 1445. The women taking part in the race set off from the church porch when the pancake bell was rung, tossing their pancakes three times during the race (while wearing an apron and a hat, or head covering). The lucky verger was entitled to kiss the winner, and the vicar gave her a prayer book.

29

A SMELLY PREDICTION

WHY St Thomas should be connected with onions in folklore is a bit of a mystery. It is nevertheless the case that in olden times people believed that on the eve of the Festival of St Thomas, 21st December, if an unmarried woman peeled an onion and wrapped it in a cloth and put it under her pillow when she went to bed, she would dream of her future husband, as long as she remembered to say the following verse:

> Good St Thomas,
> Do me right,
> Let my true love,
> Come tonight,
> That I may see him
> Face to face,
> And in my arms
> His form embrace.

PLUCK A ROSE ON CHRISTMAS DAY AT YOUR PERIL

MIDSUMMER EVE, 24th June, was maidens' night if they were looking for a husband. They were to walk backwards into the garden and pluck a rose; sew the rose up in a bag, and keep it in a bottom drawer until Christmas day. On Christmas morn the rose was taken from the bag in silence and placed by the maid in her bosom, and worn to church. If some young man asked for the rose, or even took it from her without her express leave, that man would eventually become her husband.

3

Orgy or Argy-Bargy

CHOOSE THE RIGHT DAY

Monday for wealth,
Tuesday for health,
Wednesday the best day of all;
Thursday for losses,
Friday for crosses,
And Saturday no luck at all.

WATCH THE SEASON

If you marry in Lent,
You will live to repent.

Marry in May,
Rue for aye.

WHITE GLOVES ALL ROUND

It was the custom in the sixteenth and seventeenth centuries to wear gloves at a wedding ceremony. The bride wore gloves, and gloves also had to be provided for the guests and for all the officials. Even the clergyman was presented with a pair of gloves in addition to his fee for conducting the wedding. They were always white gloves of course.

BANNED BY BANNS

Years ago it was the custom for a woman to stay away

from church when her banns were being published; it was thought that her future children ran the risk of being deaf and dumb, should she hear her banns called.

OCCUPATION COULD PROVE HAZARDOUS

STREWING the path to the church with emblems of the bridegroom's occupation was quite a common occurrence in past generations. For a carpenter there would be wood shavings; a gardener, flowers; for a farmer, cut grass; a shoemaker, bits of leather; a butcher, sheep skins, and so on.

HITCHED AT THE CHURCH DOOR

MARRIAGES were performed in the church porch until the time of Edward VI, when the ceremony was moved into the body of the church. In Anglo-Saxon times the parties to be married came to the church porch where they were met by the priest, who first blessed the ring and then gave it to the bridegroom who placed it on the middle finger of the bride's left hand. A form of blessing was recited over the couple, after which they were led into the chancel where they remained during the mass. It was in the church porch that Chaucer's Wife of Bath was wedded to the five husbands she survived—

> She was a worthy woman all her live,
> Husbands at the church dore had she five.

The old custom of 'Porch Marriages' may have been due to the fact that the wedding party came to church on horse-back. The bride and bridegroom on horseback, would be preceded by the village fiddlers as they came in procession along the lane. A long strap, held by the bridegroom, would be fastened to the bride to prevent her from falling off the horse.

MARRIAGE IN THE MIDDLE AGES

EVIDENCE from the early fifteenth century shows that before marriage, banns had to be called in the church on three solemn days, and then on the day of marriage the following form was used at the door of the church:

Priest: 'Hast thou the will to have this woman to thy wedded wife?'

Response: 'Yes, sir.'

Priest: 'Will you do your best to love her and hold to her and to no other to thy live's end?'

Response: 'Yes, sir.'

Priest: 'Then take her by your hand and say after me: I N. take thee N. in form of Holy Church to my wedded wife, forsaking all other holding myself wholly to thee, in sickness and in health, in riches and in poverty, in well and in woe, till death us depart, and thereto I plight ye my troth.'

Then the woman repeated the same form. This was 'Marriage at the Church door', and after this 'Taking to wife at the Church door', the parties entered the body of the church and completed the ceremony in the church itself. As in the case of baptisms, churchings, and funerals, the fee for marriage was fixed at 1d.

It was the custom for the bride at marriage to wear three ornaments, a ring on her finger which signified true love; a brooch on her breast, a token of the purity of heart and chastity that she ought to have; and a garland on her head, a symbol of the joy and the dignity of the Sacrament of Matrimony. The bride's veil or 'nuptual veil' as it was called was one of the items which the churchwardens were supposed to provide for the ceremony. Most parishes possessed one such veil which was used by each bride on her wedding day. In other parishes sets of jewels were sometimes loaned to the bride being married in the parish church and on occasion these were rented out to people being married in other churches.

QUICK OFF THE MARK

A WELL there is in the west-country,
    And a clearer one was never seen;
There is not a wife in the west-country
    But has heard of the well of St Keyne.

An oak and an elm-tree stand beside,
    And behind does an ash-tree grow,
And a willow from the bank above
    Droops to the water below.

A traveller came to the well of St Keyne;
    Pleasant it was to his eye,
For from cock-crow he had been travelling,
    And there was not a cloud in the sky.

He drank of the water so cool and clear,
    For thirsty and hot was he,
And he sat down under the bank,
    Under the willow tree.

There came a man from the neighbouring town
    At the well to fill his pail,
On the well-side he rested it,
    And bade the stranger hail.

'Now art thou a batchelor, stranger?' quoth he,
    'For an if thou hast a wife,
The happiest draught thou hast drank this day
    That ever thou didst in thy life.

'Or has your good woman, if one you have,
    In Cornwall ever been?
For an if she have, I'll venture my life
    She has drank of the well of St Keyne.'

'I have left a good woman who never was here,'
    The stranger he made reply;
'But that my draught should be better for that,
    I pray you answer me why.'

'St Keyne', quoth the countryman, 'many a time
    Drank of this crystal well,
And before the angel summoned her
    She laid on the water a spell.

'If the husband of this gifted well
    Shall drink before his wife,
A happy man thenceforth is he,
    For he shall be master for life.

'But if the wife should drink of it first,
    Heaven help the husband then!'

The stranger stooped to the well of St Keyne,
    And drank of the waters again.

'You drank of the well, I warrant, betimes?'
    He to the countryman said.
But the countryman smiled as the stranger spake,
    And sheepishly shook his head.

'I hastened as soon as the wedding was done,
    And left my wife in the porch.
But i' faith she had been wiser than I,
    For she took a bottle to church!'
                    Southey, 'The Well of St Keyne'

MARRIAGE BY MAGISTRATE

DURING the Commonwealth period of our nation's history couples were joined together by a magistrate. An Act of 1654 directed that no marriage could be celebrated without a certificate proving that the banns had been published three 'successive Lord's Days at the close of morning exercise, in the public meeting place, commonly called the church or chapel, or, if the parties preferred, in the market place on three successive market days'.

The pair wishing to be married took the required certificate to the Justice of the Peace, joined hands, and were married using the following formula.

'I (A B) do here, in the presence of God, the searcher of all hearts, take thee (C D) for my wedded wife, and do also, in the presence of God and before these witnesses, promise to be unto thee a loving and faithful husband'.

The woman promised to be an obedient wife and they were pronounced man and wife.

The Puritans omitted the wedding ring because of its heathen origin. Butler in his *Hudibras* ridiculed those who would banish the ring:

> Others were for abolishing
> This tool of matrimony, a ring,
> With which th' unsanctify'd Bridegroom
> Is married only to a thumb
> (As wire or ringing of a pig
> That used to break up ground and dig),
> The Bride to nothing but her will
> That nulls the after marriage still.

The Act only remained effective until 1658 when the old religious rites were allowed to be performed by those who preferred them.

RING THE LIFE-LINE

THE wedding ring was a symbol of union which would last for ever, the band having no beginning and no end. The custom of placing it on the fourth finger of the left hand was based on an ancient but mistaken idea that there is a life-line, a special artery, that goes from the heart, the 'seat of love', to that particular finger.

SPLIT-RING MARRIAGE

THE Gimmal Ring was a two hooped betrothal ring. One half was given to the girl and the other to the man: they were then joined into one for the wedding. The plain gold

37

wedding ring did not come into use until about the middle of the seventeenth century.

SPEAK UP OR SLEEP FIRST AT YOUR PERIL

IT was believed in olden days that the one who answered loudest to the question put to bride and groom by the officiating clergyman would die first. It was also believed that the first of the bridal pair to go to sleep on the wedding night would be the first to die.

A TIP FOR PARSONS

A CURIOUS custom in connection with marriage was that of giving a silver coin to the bride in the vestry immediately after the ceremony in church. Many a parson moving into areas where this was the practice thought the half-a-sovereign pressed into his hand by the bridegroom was a tip, but he was quickly put right by the bride. It was also the practice for the bride to receive the clerical salute in the form of a kiss. This too, the bride took if the parson was reluctant to give it.

POT-LUCK HOT-POTS

IT was regarded as a great honour for the newly weds in certain parts of the country in olden times if friends or neighbours sent 'hot pots' for them to sip as they left church.

Shakespeare may have had this in mind when, in *The Taming of the Shrew* he wrote:

After many ceremonies done,

He calls for wine. A health, quoth he, as if
He had been aboard carousing to his mates
After a storm; quaffed off the muscadel,
And threw the sops all in the sexton's face,
Having no other reason
But that his beard grew thin and hungerly,
And seemed to ask him sops as he was drinking.

THE WELSH WAY

IN the west part of Cardiganshire there existed well into the
nineteenth century a curious custom relating to marriage,
called 'a bidding'. This took place about a week before the
marriage ceremony. A bidder (*gwahodder*) went from house
to house in the village with a long pole to the end of which
was attached a bunch of ribbons. Standing in the middle of
the floor of each house, he addressed the householders with
great formality. He mentioned the day of the wedding, and
listed the various preparations which had been made for the
occasion. The content of the bidding varied but the formality of the custom appears to have been quite rigid. The
following specimen is given in the *Cambrian Guide*:

Araith y Gwahoddwr yn Llanbadern vawr 1762

The translation reads:

Speech of the Bidder in Llanbadern vawr 1762

The intention of the bidder is this; with kindness and
amity, with decency and liberality for Einion Owain and
Llio Elys, he invites you to come with your good will on
the plate; bring current money; a shilling, or 2, or 3, or
4, or 5; with cheese and butter we invite the husband and

wife, and children, and men-servants, from the greatest to the least. Come there early, you shall have victuals freely, and drink cheap, stools to sit on, and fish if we can catch them; but if not, hold us excusable; and they will attend on you when you call upon them in return. They set out from such a place to such a place.

The *gwahodder*, or bidder, was paid about nine shillings for his work. The marriage day was always fixed for a Saturday, and Friday was devoted to bringing home the *ystavell*, or furniture of the bride, which generally consisted of an oak chest, a feather bed, clothes and other items of linen. The bridegroom provided the bedstead, table, dresser and chairs. Friday evening was taken up with receiving presents of money, cheese and butter, at the groom's house from his friends and at the bride's house from her friends. This practice was called *pwrs a gwregys*, or purse and girdle, which seems to have been an ancient British custom. All these presents were carefully recorded on paper since if they were demanded back they were repaid.

On the Saturday the groom's friends went to his house on horseback for bread and cheese and ale and about fifteen of the best mounted went to the bride's house to demand her. The bride, still in her parents' house, was surrounded with her friends and put on an act of being unwilling to go to the wedding, whereupon abuse was hurled to and fro, the bridegroom's party outside and that of the bride inside the house.

At length the father welcomed his guests; they partook of refreshments, and proceeded to church.

The girl mounted behind her father on the swiftest horse and her friends pretended to run away with her, riding like mad in any and every direction. During this exercise the girl had no saddle and had to hold on to the man's coat. At last, when the horse had tired, the bride consented to go to church.

The ceremony being over, guests returned with the married couple to their home, eating cost free but providing their own liquor. On the Sunday the newly married pair stayed at home receiving good will and *pwython*. On Monday when the drink was exhausted the cheese was sold and on the following Sunday, most of the guests went with the newly married couple to church, and this closed the ceremony.

Nicholson's *Cambrian Guide*, 1813

THE POWER OF THE NEWLY WED'S KISS

In the North of England it was the custom to 'ride for the kail' after a wedding had taken place. The 'kail' was a smoking bowl which was filled with spiced broth. Edward Chicken, a Northumbrian poet, described it in his poem, 'The Collier's Wedding':

> Four rustic fellows wait the while,
> To kiss the bride at the church style:
> Then vig'rous mount their fettered steeds,
> With heavy heels and clumsy heads:
> They smartly scourge them head and tail
> To win what country folks call kail.

SIXPENCE FOR THE OLD MAID

There was an old-time wedding custom in the North of England where an ordinary flat cake of flour, water and currants was made, into which was placed a wedding ring and a sixpence. When the company was about to retire after the marriage festivities the cake was broken and distributed amongst the unmarried women. It was supposed that she who got the ring in her portion of the cake would shortly be married; and the one who got the sixpence would die an old maid.

ANYTHING FOR A CHANGE

IT was considered unlucky for a woman to marry a man whose surname began with the same letter as her own:

> If you change the name and not the letter,
> You change for the worse and not for the better.

AN ESSENTIAL FORE-RUNNER TO A HAPPY MARRIAGE

IN the village of Belford, Northumberland, the bridal pair were made to jump over a stone placed outside the church door. This was called the 'Couping stone', or 'Petting stone', for it was on this spot that the bride must leave behind all her pets and ill humours as she crossed the stone.

THE MARRIAGE TOUCH

TO rub shoulders with a bride or bridegroom was deemed a portent of an early marriage.

FERTILITY WISH

THE throwing of confetti (an Italian word meaning 'confections' or 'sweetmeats') in these days consists of bits of coloured paper, or real or imitation rose petals. In Victorian times rice was used and, earlier still, ears of corn. It is really a symbolic wish that the new family will have all it needs by way of children and food.

A TAP ON THE HEAD

AN old custom was for the bride's father to give the groom one of his daughter's shoes on the wedding day, showing that he was giving him authority over his daughter. The groom tapped his bride on the head with it to exercise his authority as soon as possible. If a younger daughter married before her elder sisters they were expected to dance at her wedding without their shoes.

43

YOUR MONEY OR YOUR GARTERS

A CURIOUS and somewhat daring custom used to be observed at weddings in Eccles church, if we are to judge by an account written in the early nineteenth century.

When a marriage took place at the church, on the parties leaving, the schoolmaster sent a boy or two to demand a small sum of money from the newly married couple. If they refused to give anything, he then sent more of his boys to insist upon something being given, or, if they still refused, to take the bride's garter.

The churchwardens abolished this custom in the early years of the nineteenth century, and in lieu of it, fourpence for every marriage was to be paid to the schoolmaster of Eccles, and double dues in Lent.

CURE FOR COLD FEET

LAST-MINUTE escape from the married state was made somewhat difficult in certain parishes in England in the old days. The parish accounts of Great Staughton recorded for December 1647, 'Item, paid for wages spent upon man that watched John Pickle all night till he was married 1s. od.'

WHAT SHALL WE DO WITH THE DRUNKEN GUESTS?

THE custom of imbibing too freely at wedding receptions was as common in the old days as it is now:

The fiddler did stop, and he struck up a hop,
    Whilst seated on top of a trunk,

> But not one of the batch could come up to the scratch,
>   They were all so outrageously drunk.
>   From 'Chummies Wedding' (Popular Song)

A POTTY NECKLACE

WHEN the bride entered her house for the first time a cake was broken over her head by the bridegroom's mother. Sometimes a plate of broken bread was thrown over her and if the plate got broken in the process it was considered a sign of good fortune. In some parts of the country it was the custom to put a string of crocks, or pots and pans, around the bride's neck.

The company attending the house of a newly wed couple had the joy of taking them out of doors where a basket was passed among them, and was gradually filled with stones. When it reached the bridegroom it was suspended from his neck. Thus bowed down with the weight he had to rely on his helpmate to come and cut the cord. He was then relieved of the oppressive burden in exchange for the love and caresses he would lavish on his bride.

A FINANCIAL SETTLEMENT

SAMUEL LUMB, who was eighty-three years old, was married in Halifax to Mrs Rachel Heap on the 1st October 1827. He had been married to her 25 years previously, when everyone believed her first husband to have been killed while on army service. Mr Heap returned to find her living with Mr Lumb by whom she had three children. It seems hard to believe but the menfolk involved came to terms; Mr Heap agreed to sell; Mr Lumb to buy. The lady in

45

question suffered the indignity of actually being delivered to Mr Lumb in a halter at Halifax Cross.

WIFE FOR SALE

IN Hereford Market in 1802, a butcher sold his wife by public auction for one pound and four shillings, and a bowl of punch. While the practice was illegal, it does not appear that anyone disputed the right of a husband to get rid of a wife he no longer had any use for, in this way.

A WIFE'S REQUEST

'A POORE woman's husband was to be hanged at the towne of Lancaster, and on the execution day she intreated the Shrieue to be good to her and stand her friend: the Shrieue said that he could doe her no hurt, for her husband was condemned and judged by the Law, and therefore hee must suffer. "Ah, good master Shrieue," said the woman, "it is not his life that I aske, but because I have a farre home, and my mare is old and stiffe, therefore I would intreat you to doe me the favour to let my husband be hanged first." '

Taylor's *Wit and Mirth*, 1630

MUCH MARRIED

IN *Walks in London*, Hare records that Lady Elizabeth Percy, daughter of the tenth Earl of Northumberland, was twice a widow and three times a wife before she was seventeen. She died on 27th August 1752, a Mrs Tolderoy, 'an ancient widow lady, who had buried six husbands in twenty-two years'.

4

Quaint Quackery

BLOODY BARBERS

AT the beginning of the fourteenth century the lancet was
coming into use for blood letting, and crude splints and
bandages were used. This was an age when superstition was
rampant and nearly everyone wore charms and amulets,
and belief in demons was commonplace. Barbers who practised surgery were called barber-surgeons and dentists had the
practical title of tooth drawers. When the barber-surgeon
bled his patient the 'victim' was made to grip a pole while he
was being cut. The bandage used on the patient was kept at
the shop. Barber-surgeons fixed a pole outside their premises
with an imitation bandage round it as a sign of their profession.

It was during the reign of Henry V, 1413–22, that doctors
had to be licensed before they could practise, and they had to
be enrolled as Master Surgeons. Medicine, however, was still
primitive. Stone, some thought, could be cured by a concoction of crickets' wings, beetles and oil. Red lights and red
hangings for the bed were used when patients had smallpox.

MUMMY POWDER

THE physicians of the age of Charles II, were wont to give
their patients 'mummy powder', that is, pulverised mummy.
They argued that the mummy had lasted for a very long
time, and that the patients ought to do so likewise.

DOCTOR'S DILEMMA

CRITICISM of medics is not a custom which is peculiar to our own century. An epigram on Dr Isaac *Letsome*, is most revealing:

> When peoples ill they comes to I,
>   I physics, bleeds and sweats 'em,
> Sometimes they live, sometimes they die
>   What's that to I? I Letsome.

TAKE 'A DEADMAN'S HAND' TWICE DAILY

A SOMEWHAT morbid cure for many ailments was the placing of a hand on the afflicted member. The hand was special in that in order for the cure to be effective it had to be the hand of a man who had committed suicide.

A GOLDEN CURE

Aurum potabile, or drinkable gold, was a favourite medical nostrum of the Middle Ages, because gold, being perfect, should produce perfect health.

A 'DOUBLE' ANTIDOTE

AN old cure for an adder's bite was to cut a piece of hazel-wood, and fasten a long stick to a short one to make a cross. This was laid on the wound very gently and then was said aloud:

> Underneath this hazelin mote,
> There's a Braggoty worm with a speckled throat,
>   Nine double is he:
> Now from nine double to eight double

And from eight double to seven double
And from seven double to six double
And from six double to five double
And from five double to four double
And from four double to three double
And from three double to two double
And from two double to one double
And from one double to no double
　　No double hath he!

ST PAUL'S DISEASE?

AN old cure for a thorn in the flesh was the repetition of a charm:

> Happy man that Christ was born!
> He was crowned with a thorn;
> He was pierced through the skin
> For to let the poison in:
> But his five wounds, so they say,
> Closed, before he passed away,
> In with healing, out with thorn;
> Happy man that Christ was born!

MEDICINAL PROPERTIES OF THE DONKEY

THE child with whooping cough was drawn naked nine times over the back and under the belly of a three-year-old female donkey. Three spoonsful of the donkey's milk, in which three hairs cut from the back and three from the belly of the donkey were placed, stood for three hours and was then given to the child in three doses. This was usually carried out three times to effect a complete cure.

RUPTURE REPAIRED

A YOUNG tree was split down the trunk and the ruptured person passed through the cleft. As the tree healed itself and the split was closed, so the rupture was supposed to heal. The person was usually passed through the tree in the direction of the sun and had to remain in bed until the tree grew together again. The ash and the willow were the favoured trees used for this cure.

SHORT SHARP CURES

Colic
Stand on one's head for a quarter of an hour.

Headache
Take the rope which had been used to hang a man; soak it well in water; give the sufferer a good draught of the medicine so obtained.

Anglo-Saxon headache
A salve composed of rue and mustard seed to be applied to that part of the head which was free from pain.

Teething
Hang a bag of live woodlice around baby's neck.

Baldness
Make and wear a wreath of ivy leaves.

Breathing complaints
Put the lung of a fox into sweetened wine and drink the mixture.

Hiccough
Wet the forefinger of the right hand with spittle and cross the front of the left shoe three times, repeating the Lord's Prayer backwards.

Rheumatism
Crawl under a bramble which has formed a second root in the ground. Or get a woman who has been delivered of a child feet foremost, to tread the patient.

Bite of a mad Anglo-Saxon dog
Take two or three onions, boil them, spread them in ashes, mix them with fat and honey, lay them on.

Whooping cough
Tie round the child's neck a hairy caterpillar in a small bag.
As the insect dies the cough diminishes.

Measles
During the reign of Charles I, a live sheep laid on a patient's
bed was thought to be the cure for measles.

Cramp

> Cramp, be thou faintless,
> As our Lady was sinless,
> When she bore Jesus.

Pepys

PARSON SOUP

EVEN until midway through the nineteenth century people
were in the habit of taking from graveyards portions of
clay from a priest's grave. This was used as a cure for many
diseases, on occasions boiling the clay to make soup for those
who were sick.

DEAD CERTAIN CURE

A VARIETY of cures for warts and boils and skin disorders
were associated with visits to newly made graves in churchyards and cemeteries. It was an old custom that a dead
person's tooth carried in the pocket was a certain cure for
toothache.

MONUMENTAL PRESCRIPTION

THE lack of fingers and noses on so many alabaster effigies
on old tombs is due to the strange custom of obtaining
small pieces of alabaster and grinding them down to powder

in order to concoct a mixture which was believed to be a cure for the 'King's Evil'.

ANOTHER USE FOR MISTLETOE

APART from being a good general tonic, mistletoe tea was believed to be a cure for epilepsy and a preventative against all nervous illness. 'A few of the berries of the mistletoe bruised and strained into oyle and drunken' was the remedy given by the herbalist, Johnson.

SLIM THE EASY WAY

> KISS the black cat,
> An' 'twill make ye fat;
> Kiss the white one,
> 'Twill make ye lean.

MANICURE FORECAST

CUT them on Monday, you cut them for health;
Cut them on Tuesday, you cut them for wealth;
Cut them on Wednesday, you cut them for news;
Cut them on Thursday, a new pair of shoes;
Cut them on Friday, you cut them for sorrow;
Cut them on Saturday, see your true love tomorrow;
Cut them on Sunday, the devil will be with you all
   the week.

EVERY MOTHER KNOWS

FRONTLETS were known to every good wife: 'rose-water and vinegar, with a little woman's milk, and nutmegs grated upon a rose-cake applied to both temples.' It was also believed that, 'peony doth cure epilepsy; precious stones most diseases; a wolf's dung borne with one helps the colic, a spider an ague.'

The Revd Robert Burton says that: 'at Lindley in Leicestershire, my father's house, I first observed this amulet of a spider in a nut-shell lapped in silk, etc., so applied for an ague by my mother.'

SLEEP TIGHT: SWEET DREAMS

'SACKS of wormwood, mandrake, henbane, roses made like pillows and laid under the patient's head' were thought to ensure a sound sleep, while in order to prevent bad dreams, patients were urged 'to anoint the soles of the feet with the fat of a dormouse, the teeth with ear-wax of a dog, swine's gall, hare's ears.'

Carden

STONE THE PATIENTS

IN Scotland, stones shaped like various parts of the human body were expected to cure the diseases with which these members were afflicted. These stones were called by the names of the limbs which they represented, as 'eye-stone', 'head-stone'. The patient washed the affected part of the body, and rubbed it well with the stone corresponding.

Gregor, *Folk Lore of North East Counties*

'WHEN TAKEN, TO BE WELL SHAKEN'

THE commonplace book of a noble Sussex squire, dated 1672, contains the following specimens of the domestic treatment of certain disorders:

To cure the whooping cough—
'Get three field mice, flaw them, draw them and roast

one of them, and let the party afflicted eat it; dry the other two in the oven until they crumble to a powder, and put a little of this powder in what the patient drinks at night and in the morning.'

The next recipe is headed 'to cure the stone, though of long standing':

'Take a hedgehog, and kill him, and flaw him, and wash the skin very clean, and then spread it out with something that will keep it at its full length. So stretched, dry it in the oven until the prickles will come off, which take and beat to a powder and take the same powder in whatever liquid you drink'.

R. Thurston Hopkins *Old English Mills and Inns*, 1927

BISHOP QUACK

DORA H. ROBERTSON in her book *Sarum Close* (published by Forecrest Publishing Limited, Bath) records that Bishop Seth Ward of Salisbury, who died in 1689, left behind after his death notebooks with a collection of quack remedies, and one which savours strongly of witchcraft.

Unguentum Podagricum (for gout)—'Take an old fat cat, and flea it, draw forth the gutts, then with a rolling pin beat it well, and so put it all together into the Belly of a fat Gander with pepper ½lb. Mustard and Parsley Seeds ℥ iiij six-penny weight of Bole Armoniac, a good quantity of Wormwood, Rue (and Garlick) Rost the Gander wel, saving the greas, with it anoint the grieved part.'

SHINGLE BELLS

AN old cure for shingles was the green moss which accumulated on church bells when they had long been exposed to the damp air. This was scraped off the bell and rubbed on the infected area of the body.

DEVILISH NUMBERS

THE most devilish thing is 8 times 8 and 7 times 7; it is what nature itself can't endure

Marjorie Fleming

In the Register of Bedworth, Warwickshire for the year 1719 there is an entry which states, 'We declare our judgement against the evil of our members going to be touched by a seventh son in order to cure diseases, and then wearing the silver he gives them'. The old custom was that the seventh son was born to a be physician with the charismatic gift of healing by touch alone.

The silver charm mentioned is also interesting as a development of this custom is widespread even today. At the birth of a seventh son the first thing his hands touched gave him the power to heal. Salt or meal or silver was always, therefore, close at hand.

WITCHCRAFT PREVENTION

No exorciser harm thee!
Nor no witchcraft charm thee!

Cymbeline, IV. ii

According to a manuscript on magic preserved in the Chetham Library, Manchester, 'the herb pimpernell is good to prevent witchcraft, as Mother Bumby doth affirme', and the following lines must be used when it is gathered:

Herbe pimpernell, I have thee found
Growing upon Christ Jesus' ground:
The same gifte the Lord Jesus gave unto thee,
When he shed his blood on the tree.
Arise up, pimpernell, and goe with me,
And God blesse me,
And all that shall were thee. Amen.

'Say this fifteen dayes together, twice a day, morning earlye
fasting, and in the evening full.'

SEWAGE DISPOSAL OF WITCHES

WHEN animals or humans had been bewitched it was
commonly believed that if a bottle of urine from the
diseased beast or person was buried neck downwards, the
witch would be afflicted with *strangury*, and in her suffering
confess her crime and beg forgiveness.

TOOTH PROTECTION

IT was an old custom for a person in the parish of Llanelli,
South Wales, to bury in the old churchyard any dislodged
tooth so as to ensure protection from haunting by spirits of
the dead.

ST PETER TO THE RESCUE

PETER was sitting on a marble-stone,
    And Jesus passed by;
Peter said, 'My Lord, my God,
    How my tooth doth ache!'
    Jesus said, 'Peter art whole!

And whoever keeps these words for my sake
Shall never have tooth-ache.'

EPISCOPAL DIAGNOSIS

BEDE tells the following story: 'Once upon a time, John, Bishop of York came to the monastery of Virgins, at the place called Wetadum (Walton, Yorkshire) where the Abbess Hereberga then presided.

When we were come thither and had been received with great and universal joy, the abbess told us that one of the virgins, who was her daughter in the flesh, laboured under a grievous distemper, having been lately bled in the arm, and whilst she was engaged in study, was seized with a sudden violent pain, which increased so that the wounded arm became worse, and so much swelled that it could not be grasped with both hands; and thus being confined to her bed, she was expected to die very soon. The abbess entreated the bishop that he would vouchsafe to go in and give her his blessing, for that she believed that she would be better for his blessing or touching her. He asked when the maiden had been bled; and being told that it was on the fourth day of the moon, said: 'You did very indiscreetly and unskilfully to bleed her on the fourth day of the moon; for I remember that Archbishop Theodorus, of blessed memory, said, that bleeding at that time was very dangerous, when the light of the moon and the tide of the ocean are increasing; and what can I do to the girl if she is like to die.'

APOSTOLIC AID

COLERIDGE in his 'Table Talk' records the custom of

dealing with cramp in Christ's Hospital. The schoolboy when attacked by cramp would stand firmly on the affected leg, and make the sign of the cross over it, repeating the following formula three times:

The devil is tying a knot in my leg,
Matthew, Mark, Luke and John unloose it, I beg;
Crosses three we make to ease us,
Two for the thieves, and one of Christ Jesus.

WART REMOVAL

MANY and varied are the traditional cures for warts. One was to take a large snail, rub the wart well with it, and throw the poor thing against a wall or better still, against a thorn hedge. As the snail rotted on the bush, so, it was believed, would the wart disappear.

Hunt records how the Vicar of Bodmin found, not long ago, a bottle full of pins laid in a newly dug grave. This is evidence of the practice of touching each wart with a new pin, which was then dropped into a bottle. The bottle was then placed either in a newly dug grave or buried in earth at a crossroads. As the pin rusted the warts were presumed to disappear.

Another cure for warts was to take a length of string, tie as many knots in it as there were warts to cure, then each wart was touched with a knot which was then considered dedicated to it. The string was then buried and as it rotted so the warts fell away from the body.

The pebble cure consisted of rubbing each wart with a

pebble, then these were placed in a bag and 'lost' on the way to church.

Some people believed that a piece of meat 'stolen' from a butcher's rubbed on warts and subsequently buried would cure them. As the meat rotted the warts disappeared.

LET INDIGESTION NOT VEX HIM

> HICCUP, snick up,
> Rise up, right up,
> Three drops in a cup,
> Are good for the hiccup.

BLESS YOU

SNEEZE on Monday, sneeze for danger,
Sneeze on Tuesday, kiss a stranger,
Sneeze on Wednesday, receive a letter,
Sneeze on Thursday, something better,
Sneeze on Friday, sneeze for sorrow,
Sneeze on Saturday, see your true love tomorrow,
Sneeze on Sunday, your safety seek,
Or the devil will have you for the rest of the week.

Some versions end:

> Sneeze on Sunday morning fasting
> Enjoy your true love for everlasting.

FIRE-FIGHTING WORDS

To cure burns it was customary to recite:

Two angels from the North,
One brought fire, the other brought frost.

Out fire,
    In frost,
In the name of Father, Son and Holy Ghost!

RELIGIOUS CAUTERISATION

BLOOD was staunched by intoning:

Christ was born in Bethlehem;
Baptised in the river Jordan.
The river stood,—
So shall thy blood,
John Jones (or whatever the person's name was),
In the name of the Father,
And of the Son,
And of the Holy Ghost, Amen!

SKIN CRAFT

IN order to cure a skin complaint the following recitation
should be intoned on Midsummer Day:

St John Baptist,
    Good in,
    Evil out,
Itch out too.

A TOUCH OF THE 'ROYALS'

IT was a widespread belief that the 'royal touch' could cure
scrofula (otherwise known as the King's Evil), without any
medicine save that of handling and prayers. But before
anyone could be presented for this privilege he had to
receive a certificate from the parson of his parish to the

effect that he had never been touched before. Hambledon Register, Bucks, 17th May 1685 records that:

> Mary Wallington had a certificate to goe before the King for a disease called the King's Evil.

Hundreds were touched for scrofula. The king crossed the sores with a coin, known as an angel noble, which was hung round the sufferer's neck.

'EELED ALCOHOLICS'

IN time past the eel was said to possess the power of enforcing sobriety upon the most devoted subject.

> If you would make some notorious drunkard to loathe and abhorre his beastly vice, and for ever after to hate the drinking of wine, put an eel alive, into some wyde-mouthed bottle with a cover, having in it, such a quantity of wine, as may suffice of itself, to suffocate and strangle the eel; which done, take out the dead eel, and let the partie whom you would have reclaymed, not knowing hereof, drink of that wine only as much as he listeth.

5

The Demon Drink

A BASE, UNWORTHY INDIAN CUSTOM

WHEN tea and coffee were first introduced into England they were, to say the least, unpopular beverages. Tea in particular was thought to undermine the strength of a man and the beauty of women. Even as late as the end of the eighteenth century some physicians were still attacking the tea and coffee 'habit'. One such remarked that they 'are permitted by God's providence for lessening the number of mankind by shortening life, as a kind of silent plague'.

It was at Buckingham Palace that the first cup of tea was brewed and drunk. The house was then the residence of the Duke of Buckingham. He it was who brought the first tea into England, and invited a group of friends to taste the decoction which he himself had brewed.

NO STRONG DRINK

'Now therefore beware, I pray thee, and drink no cider nor strong drink!' Judges 13. 4. (fourteenth century translation of the Bible by Wycliffe and Nicholas de Hereford).

The custom of drinking brandy came into England from the Continent and became so popular that in 1673 Parliament was petitioned to forbid the importing of brandy, tea and coffee on the ground that their popularity was seriously injuring the home-grown products such as barley and malt. For a short time it was illegal to import brandy.

> If all be true that I do think,
> There are five reasons we should drink:
> Good wine—a friend—or being dry—
> Or lest we should be, by and by—
> Or any other reason why!
>
> Henry Aldrich, Dean of Christ Church, 1647–1710

LIQUID REFRESHMENT SUNDAY

THE fourth Sunday in Lent is also known as Refreshment Sunday. The Gospel for the day is the story of the feeding of the five thousand and the lesson for Evensong is about Joseph's liberality to his father and brothers.

'And they drank, and were merry with him.' The Authorised Version includes the extra information: 'They drank, drank largely.' This gave rise to another name for the feast, Bragget Sunday. This name is probably Celtic in origin; the Welsh *bragawd*, or mead, was the term for the popular British drink in which honey was used as a base.

MEAD BY THE BATHFUL

SWEET is old wine in bottles, ale in barrels, mead in bathfuls.

Some villages in Wales where people often had to pay rentals in kind to the prince, had to provide a certain measure of mead. In the old laws it was laid down that the mead should be brought to the prince's palace and poured into a vat, big enough to allow the prince and the village elder to bathe together without bumping each other!

THIRSTY DAYS

THIRSTY days, hath September

April, June and November;
All the rest are thirsty too
Except for him who hath home brew

Climatic conditions in England led to the custom of ale drinking as vine cultivation was impossible. The art of brewing developed quickly and by the year 1200 a Guild of Brewers existed in London. Most of the brewing, however, was done by the women-folk. Many varieties of ale were brewed but the normal drink was thin ale, which was consumed as soon as it was ready; the thick ale, 'podyng', was kept for some time in open vessels before it touched the lips. On occasions the ale was spiced or pepper was added to give it a bite, which gave rise to the practice of calling it 'stingo'.

INTRODUCTION OF HOPS

Hops, reformation, bays and beer,
Came into England all in a year

Hops were introduced into England from Germany in the reign of Henry VIII and the word bier, or beer, then came into common use.

THE TROUSERS TEST

IN olden days ale-testers were employed to determine whether or not the drink was good and wholesome. In spite of the many adulterations which were employed in brewing, the only impurity tested for was sugar. The ale-tester, wearing leather breeches would enter an inn, draw a glass of ale, pour a little of it on a bench, and sit in the puddle for 30 minutes. He would not change his position in any way and at the end of the half-hour the test was made;

E

he would attempt to rise from his seat. If the ale was impure the sugar would ensure that his breeches stuck to the bench; if sugar was absent no impression would be made on them.

XXX

THE marking of beer barrels with the symbols x, xx, and xxx is a custom which owes its origin to the monastic office of cellarer. Monastic ale was some of the best available in olden days and to ensure that the reputation was upheld the barrels were marked as a guarantee that the ale was wholesome and of good quality. It is likely that the symbol in its original form was that of a crucifix and x gradually became a form of trade mark.

A BINDING MIXTURE

THERE was an old custom in some parts of the country whereby hot ale was used to mix mortar since it was thought to give the mortar durability.

The records of the parish of Ecclesfield (South Yorkshire) for 1619 include this item:

> Itm. For 11 gallands of strong
> liquor for the blending
> of the lyme—iijs. viijd.

Not only was 'strong liquor' used to blend the lime, it was also consumed in fair quantity by the workmen. A record for 1621 shows:

> For sixe gallons of ale whc.
> we bestowed of the workmen
> whilst they was pointing steeple—ijs.

Bess of Hardwicke, the lady responsible for erecting several stately houses, including Hardwick and Chatsworth, was supposed to have been told by a fortune-teller that she would only live as long as she continued to build. Perhaps it was significant that she died in the time of the severe frost of 1607 when the workmen could not continue building even though they tried to mix their mortar with hot ale.

FUND-RAISING FUN

'CHURCH ale' was an old custom in many country parishes in time past. It was a festival kept to honour the saint of the church's dedication and also to raise money for the upkeep of the fabric of the church. This custom existed before church-rates were levied for the purpose.

It was the business of the churchwardens to brew a considerable quantity of strong ale which the parishioners not only bought but paid over the odds for. It became a method of soliciting gifts for the church fund.

> The Churches much owe, as we all do know,
> For when they be drooping and ready to fall,
> By a Whitsun or Church-ale up again they shall go
> And owe their repairing to a pot of good ale.
>
> Francis Beaumont

In certain townes where dronken Bacchus beares swaie against Christmas and Easter, Whitsondaie, or some other tyme, the churchwardens of every parishe, with the consent of the whole parishe, provide halfe a score or twenty quarters of mault, whereof some they buy of the churche stocke, and some is given them of the parishioners themselves, everyone conferring somewhat according to his abilitie; which mault being made into very strong ale or beere, is sette for sale either in the church, or some other place assigned for that purpose. Then, when this is set abroche, well is he that can gette the soonest to it, and spend the most at it. In this kinde of practice they continue six weekes, a quarter of a yeare, yea, halfe a year together. That money, they say, is to repair their churches and chappels with; to buy bookes for service; cuppes for the celebration of the Sacrament; surplesses for Sir John, and such other necessaries. And they maintain other extraordinarie charges in their parish besides.

Stubbes, Anatomy of Abuses, 1585

DRINKING AND BURYING

THEY gave him a lovely funeral. It took six men to carry the beer.

Schoolboy's essay on the Duke of Wellington

Eating, drinking and burying were closely connected in olden times. A great deal of importance was attached to funeral frolics by our ancestors. One, Margaret Atkinson, by her will, 18th October 1544, ordered that,

> the next Sunday after her burial, there be provided two dozens of bread, a kilderkin of ale, two gammons of bacon, three shoulders of mutton, and two couple of rabbits, desiring all the parish, as well rich as poor, to take part thereof, and a table to be set in the midst of the church, with everything necessary thereto.

Jefferson's Book of the Clergy

GOD SEND THIS CRUM-WELL DOWN

VISITING Lancashire in 1671 the king found that the Puritan magistrates had unlawfully punished people for having their lawful holiday fun. In 1672 he issued a declaration about merry-making and sport, such as Morris-dances, May-games, Whitsun-ales, and the setting up of May-poles. 'If these be taken away from the meaner sort, who labour hard all the week,' said the declaration, 'they will have no recreations at all to refresh their spirits; and in place thereof it will set up filthy tipplings and drunkenness and breed a number of idle and discontented speeches in their ale-houses.' The king also believed it would 'hinder the conversation of many, whom their priests will take occasion hereby to vex, persuading them that no honest mirth or recreation is lawfully tolerable in our religion'.

CHURCH ALE

> GOD is pleased when we depart from sin,
> The Devil's pleased when we persist therein

Ben Jonson

Like most customs 'Church ale' in the course of time was abused.

The Canons of 1683 ruled that 'the Churchwardens or questmen and their assistants shall suffer no plays, feasts, banquets, supper, Church-ale drinkings . . . in the Church, Chapels or Churchyard.'

This ruling took the custom of Church ale away from the church itself and there are isolated instances recorded in certain parishes where the practice went 'underground'. During the 'beating of the bounds' a hole was dug, and the men used to jump into it and drink as much as they could; whether they ever got out of the hole is not recorded.

GIN DISPENSER

DRUNK for a penny, dead drunk for twopence.

A wave of 'gin fever' swept the country in the last decade of the seventeenth century and because gin was so cheap to produce it challenged beer as the national beverage. So much poverty, vice and misery came with it that the Government passed the Gin Act of 1736, heavily taxing the spirit and compelling the retailer to take out a £50 licence.

The gin-drinking custom had become so established that the minds of men were put to evading the severe legislation. One illicit drinking establishment in London at this time was the forerunner of the automatic dispensing machine which is commonplace today: at the sign of the Old Tom Cat, the gin drinker, by dropping his penny into a slot of the figure of the cat, would get his money's worth of spirit from the end of a pipe concealed in the cat's paw.

DRINKING SESSION

I HAVE very poor and unhappy brains for drinking.

Othello, II. iii.

The custom of visiting a neighbouring village for a 'drinking session' was not uncommon in olden days. Tradition has it that Shakespeare, with a party of his companions, went to the old Falcon Inn at Bidford to drink ale and play shovel-board. There was a Whitsun-ale at Bidford and young Shakespeare and his companions accepted a challenge to try their prowess in ale-drinking against a party of Bidford men. The men of Bidford proved the strongest, and the losers endeavoured to return to Stratford. Their potations had been so deep, however, that they had to rest on the roadside, under a crab apple tree, little more than a mile from Bidford; here they slept from Saturday evening till Monday morning, when they were awakened by some labourers going to work. His companions entreated him to return and renew the contest, but Shakespeare refused, exclaiming, 'No, I have had enough; I have drinked with

> Piping Pebworth, dancing Marston,
> Haunted Hillbro', hungry Grafton,
> Drudging Exhall, papish Wicksford,
> Beggarly Broom, and drunken Bidford.'

These villages can be seen from the spot where this event is supposed to have taken place.

RUM AND GROG

> FIFTEEN men on the dead man's chest
> Yo-ho-ho and a bottle of Rum.
>
> Stevenson

About the middle of the seventeenth century a drink named Kill-Devil was introduced into England's ships trading in the West Indies. Rumbullion, or rum as it grew to be known, became the drink of the Navy and each sailor got a ration of half a pint a day. It was not until 1724 that Admiral Vernon, 'Old Grog', as he was called, changed the practice and introduced grog, which was a mixture of half spirit and half water.

Rum drinking was thought to lead to violence but there were old-time judges who defended the custom. One such was Lord Hermand. When a case came before him of a man charged with stabbing another to death, his direction to the jury revealed his bias.

> They had been carousing the whole night and yet he stabbed him. After drinking a whole bottle of rum with

71

him. Good God! If he will do this when he is drunk, what will he do when he's sober?

IN-KEEPING

In 1684, Archbishop Leighton died in his favourite inn, 'The Bell', in Warwick Lane, London. Gilbert Burnet, the historian, recorded that the Archbishop said that if he had to select a place to die in it should be an inn, it looked like a pilgrim going home.

DEGREES OF THIRST

To drink is a Christian diversion
Unknown to the Turk or the Persian.

Congreve

Knowles in describing the daily life of the monastery says;

When a single meal was the norm for more than half the year the need was naturally felt for a refreshing drink which in an age before tea and coffee, could be no other than beer or wine. The evening drink was of very early institution, as was also the *caritas* of wine at the *Mandatum*; an afternoon drink in summer at what is now tea-time was likewise recognised even by the exacting Pecham (Glastonbury 1281). There was, however, a tendency, as in all large establishments of every age, for one refreshing drink to succeed another, and reformers were busy at the upas-tree.

During the middle of the eighth century an attempt was made to effect cathedral reform. The rules laid down for the cathedral clergy concerning their dietary were generous as they were engaged in active life. They were permitted to

72

eat flesh and to drink wine and beer; to presbyters and deacons three cups were allowed at dinner, and two at supper; for sub-deacons two at each meal; for the servants two at dinner and one at supper. This arrangement took for granted that a presbyter would be more thirsty than a sub-deacon, and he than a serving man.

LEAD US NOT INTO TEMPTATION

IF any monk through drinking too freely get thick of speech, so that he cannot join in the psalmody, he is to be deprived of his supper.

Gildas, AD 570

At the Synod convened by Cuthbert in 747 which met at Cloveshoo, monastics and ecclesiastics were warned against drunkenness:

> Nor let them force others to drink intemperately, but let their entertainments be cleanly and sober, not luxurious nor with any mixture of delicacies or scurrilities, lest the reverence due to their habit grow into contempt and deserve infamy among seculars; and that, unless some necessary infirmity compel them, they do not, like common tipplers, help themselves or others to drink, till the canonical, that is, the ninth hour, be fully come.

In addition, monks were especially enjoined not to 'imitate seculars in the customary gartering of their legs, nor in having shags about their heads, after the fashion of the laymans cloak, contrary to the custom of the Church.'

FREE DRINKER

THE Abbott of Burton brewed good ale,

On Fridays when they fasted—
But the Abbot of Burton never tasted his own
As long as his neighbour's lasted.

PRIEST AND PUB

YE shall not keep nor suffer to be kept in your parsonage
or vicarage house, tippling houses or taverns, nor shall ye
sell ale, beer or wine.

Bishop Grindle, *Injunction to the Clergy*, 1572

The connection between the local parish church and the
inn in olden days was very close. From time to time it was
too close for comfort. The Revd Mr Carter, curate of
Lastingham in the eighteenth century, whose stipend was
£20, ran a public house to help support his wife and 13
children. His archdeacon on one occasion took him to task,
and he pleaded his case thus:

It is true that my wife keeps a public house, but as my
parish is so wide that some of my parishioners have to
come ten to fifteen miles to church, you will readily allow
that some refreshment before they return must occasionally be necessary, and when can they have it more properly
than when their journey is half performed. Now, sir,
from your own general knowledge of the world I make
no doubt but you are well assured that the most general
topics in conversation at public houses are politics and
religion, with which ninety-nine out of one hundred of
those who participate in the general clamour are totally
unacquainted; and that perpetually ringing in the ears of
a pastor, who has the welfare and happiness of his flock
at heart, must be no small mortification. To divert their

attention from these foibles over their cups, I take down my violin and play them a few tunes, which gives me an opportunity of seeing that they get no more liquor than necessary for refreshment; and if the young people propose a dance, I seldom answer in the negative; nevertheless, when I announce time for return, they are ever ready to obey my commands, and generally with the donation of a sixpence they shake hands with my children, and bid God bless them. Thus my parishioners enjoy a triple advantage, being instructed, fed and amused at the same time.

S. Baring-Gould, *Yorkshire Oddities*, 1874

GIVEN TO THE POOR

HE who drinks alone is unworthy to love.

Theophile Gautier

There was an ancient custom for the rector of Piddle Hinton, Dorsetshire, to give away, on old Christmas day, annually, a pound of bread, a pint of ale, and a mince pie, to every poor person in the parish.

ENTOMBED SPIRITS

THERE have been times when many sea-side churches on the coast of England were used as storage places for contraband liquor. The church was probably thought to be a good hiding place since few of them were used by the general public except on Sundays.

Even the churchyards were put into use by the smuglers, and many an ancient tomb has opened mysteriously and uncannily at dead of night to emit spirits of a very

75

different nature from those accredited to the abode of the departed.

A. Hyatt Verrill, *Smugglers and Smuggling*

NO DRINKS DURING SERVICE

THOU shalt not tipple in licensed premises during divine service.

Before the policing of rural areas, the only supervision of licensed premises was carried out by the ecclesiastic authorities, usually in the persons of the churchwardens. It was the custom in certain areas for the wardens, led by the verger, to leave church on Sunday mornings before the reading of the second lesson to visit the taverns and licensed houses of the district. Anyone found tippling was immediately placed in the stocks.

THE BARREL PUNISHMENT

OH, he was a genial smiling man
And fond of whisky plain;
But when he joined the temperance club
He never smiled again.

Anon

In Newcastle-on-Tyne, there was a unique punishment for people charged with extreme drunkenness: it was known as the 'drunkard's cloke'. This consisted of a barrel which had openings for the head, arms and legs, and in this cumbersome garb the culprit was led around the town to the jeers and insults of the inhabitants.

MODERATION IN ALL THINGS

THE Order of Temperance, founded in 1600 by the Landgrave of Hesse, did not have rules which the members would find impossible to keep: they were expected to undertake to drink no more than seven glasses of alcoholic refreshment at any one time, and they were required to limit their drinking to twice a day.

FOR JOY AND JUPITER

WINE was created from the beginning to make men joyful and not to make them drunk.

Ecclesiasticus, 31

The ancients took three cups: one to allay thirst; another for pleasure; and a third as a libation to Jupiter Servator, or to the drinker's favourite deity.

DRINK UP OR ELSE

'IF any person refused to drink the liquor assigned to him, or committed any offence against the convivial customs at the festive gatherings for which this ancient manor (Haddon Hall, Derbyshire) was so famous, his wrist was locked in an upright position in the iron ring, and the liquor he had declined, or else a quantity of cold water, was poured down the sleeve of his doublet.'

W. Andrews, *Bygone Punishments*

NOT TO BE WASTED

DRUNKENNESS is better for the body than physic, because there be more old drunkards than old physicians.

Rabelais

Here's to temperance,
We drink it again,
But plague take the men
Who from liquor abstain.
We do not force on him our drink,
For it would be a crime
To pour good liquor down a sink
And waste the brewer's time.

A HAIR OF THE DOG!

WE bore him home and put him to bed
And we told his wife and daughter
To give him, next morning, a couple of red
Herrings with soda water.

Ingoldsby Legends

ADVICE TO PUBLICANS

'HE (the publican) must try to emulate the example of a man whom I have heard, who was a churchwarden for seventeen years and still remained a Christian. His patience must be beyond that of an ass.'

Alexander Pratt, *Art and Practice of Innkeeping*

DEAD KEEN ON HIS OCCUPATION

THERE was at one time an eccentric landlord who kept the Castle at Stevenage. Through a clause in his will, he directed that his body should remain on the premises after his death, and accordingly his coffin was placed across the rafters of the stable.

'A GOOD WINE NEEDS NO BUSH'

THE custom of inn signs has its origin in antiquity. Certainly the Romans named their streets from the sign of the main wineshop in them. The earliest sign for an inn was a bunch of evergreens and this became the accepted symbol for a house of refreshment. Before the days of licensing, when anyone could sell alcoholic beverages without obtaining a licence from the magistrates, it was the custom to place a bush over the doorway of such a house to inform the passer-by that drink was available for purchase. Over the years the language of the inn sign has evolved. Perhaps one of the most interesting on record is the 'Five Alls' showing a King (I rule all), a Lawyer (I plead for all), a Bishop (I pray for all), a Soldier (I fight for all), and a Working man (I pay for all).

ORIGIN OF THE 'TIP'

PASS the hat for your credit's sake, and pay-pay-pay.

Rudyard Kipling

It was an old custom in coaching inns to have a box set out in a prominent position for the customers to put gratuities in for the staff. This custom 'To Insure Promptitude', led to the initials TIP being printed on the gratuity box and the monies obtained in this way became known as 'the tip'.

A TIPPLING TIP

DEAN SWIFT in his satire 'Directions to Servants,' directs the butler:

If anyone calls for small beer towards the end of the dinner, do not give yourself the trouble of going down to the cellar, but gather the droppings and leavings out of the several cups and glasses, and salvers into one; but turn your back to the company, for fear of being observed. On the contrary, when anyone calls for ale towards the end of dinner, fill the largest tankard cup topful, by which you will have the greatest part left to oblige your fellow-servants without the sin of stealing from your master.

DRINKING SONGS

I HAVE no pain, dear mother, now,
But oh! I am so dry;
Connect me to a brewery
And leave me there to die.

The custom of 'drinking songs' is as old as beer drinking itself and such songs were as popular in the village fairs of olden times as they were in the music halls of the Victorian era. It is said that on one occasion Queen Victoria herself was listening to a regimental band on the terrace of Windsor Castle when she heard an unfamiliar tune. She asked the bandmaster for its title. 'Come,' was his reply, 'it's one of those common music-hall songs.' 'What are the words?' demanded her Majesty. Gulping a little he stammered,

'Come where the booze is cheaper,
Come where the pots hold more;
Come where the boss is a bit of a joss,
Come to the pub next door.'

TOAST THAT PLEASES MOST

THE term 'toast' comes from the time before hops were used to give ale its piquancy and it was the practice to sharpen its flavour with toasted bread or a roasted crab apple.

The following song has been attributed to Bishop Still and also John Bridges, Bishop of Oxford:

Back and side go bare go bare,
    Both foot and hand go cold;
But, belly, God send thee good ale enough,
    Whether it be new or old.

I love roast but a nut-brown toast,
 And crab laid in the fire;
A little bread shall do me stead,
 Much bread I not desire.

DRINK TO THE LADIES

HERE's to the maiden of bashful fifteen,
Here's to the widow of fifty,
Here's to the flaunting extravagant queen,
Here's to the housewife that's thrifty:
Let the toast pass, drink to the lass,
I warrant she'll prove an excuse for the glass.

Sheridan

While it is claimed that the first recorded instance of drinking healths in England was in AD 450 at a feast given by King Vortigern of Britain to his Saxon allies when Rowena was the subject of his attention, the origin of the toast is somewhat more amusing.

In the days of Charles II, in the city of Bath, a celebrated beauty of that city was in the Cross Bath when one of the men in the crowd of admirers took a glass of the water in which she was standing and drank her health to the assembled crowd. In the crowd was a fellow, gay and well laced, who offered to jump in, and swore, 'though he liked not the liquor, he would have the toast'. While his ardour was held in check his *bon mot* became the origin of the raising of glasses in what has ever since been termed a toast.

HERE'S TO THE OLD COW

THE custom of toasting the oxen on New Year's Day by

the farm-hands was done in beer, the best specimen of the herd being selected for the honour.

Here is to you, Champion, with your white horn.
God send our master a good crop of corn.
Both wheat, rye, and barley and all sorts of grain,
If we meet this time twelvemonth we'll drink to him again.
Thee eat thy pousse, and I'll drink my beer,
And the Lord send us a Happy New Year.

BACK TO FRONT

I wish I were a brewer's horse,
  Five quarters of the year,
I'd place my head where was my tail
  And drink up all the ale.

There was an old rural custom of 'shoeing the colt'. When a colt was brought in to the blacksmith to be shod for the first time a number of the villagers and farmers would gather at the forge to witness the event. After the operation the company would retire to the inn where they would 'wet the shoes', in good ale, toasting the colt and wishing its owner good fortune.

ACT OF LOVE

I stabb'd mine arm to drink her health
The more fool I. The more fool I.

Old Song

After the Reformation the custom of pledging in alcoholic beverages became common, especially where young gallants and ladies were concerned. The practice of the former was to toast their mistresses kneeling, and to stab themselves, usually in the arm, mingle their blood with the wine and declare their undying love.

HORNY OATH

POPHAM, in his *Old London Customs*, claims that at the Gatehouse in Highgate the 'Highgate Oath' had to be taken by the visitor. The poor unfortunate had to 'swear on the horns' (a pair of horns attached to a long stick) never to kiss the maid when he had the opportunity of kissing the mistress, never to drink small beer when he could get strong, and never to eat brown bread when he could eat white.

GLASS DISTINCTION

IN olden times it was the custom for people to scratch their names on the window of the inn where they took their refreshment. In order for this to be effectively done, a diamond had to be used. This practice resulted in the following sour comment being inscribed on the window of one inn.

> Should you ever chance to see
> A man's name writ on glass,
> Be sure he owns a diamond,
> And his parents own an ass.

6

Ecclesiastical Antics

RECTORY RIOTS

THERE was an old custom in the parish of Drayton Beau-
champ, Buckinghamshire, called 'Stephening'. On St
Stephen's Day all the inhabitants of the parish went to the
rectory to eat as much bread and cheese, and drink as much
ale as they wanted, at the expense of the rector. This custom
ceased about the year 1827 due to 'much rioting' at the
rectory.

THE POOR CURATE

I WAS a pale young curate then.

W. S. Gilbert

In the days when pluralism was rife in the Church of
England a few favoured ecclesiastics had livings showered
on them. They visited their parishes once a year, but in
order to claim their tithe they put the unfortunate parish
in the charge of a curate who received a stipend of £20 or
£30 a year, while they, the rectors, deans and canons, holding
many livings under the system of pluralism, counted their
income in hundreds. A parson of the Hanoverian period,
Dr Syntax, was described thus by Combe:

> Of Church-preferment he had none;
> Nay, all his hope of that was gone:
> He felt that he content must be

With drudging in a curacy.
Indeed, on ev'ry Sabbath-day,
Through eight long miles he took his way,
To preach, to grumble and to pray;
To cheer the good, to warn the sinner,
And, if he got it—eat a dinner:
To bury these, to christen those,
And marry such fond folks as chose
To change the tenor of their life,
And risk the matrimonial strife.
Thus were his weekly journeys made,
'Neath summer suns and wintry shade;
And all his gains, it did appear,
Were only thirty pounds a-year.

And when he died

The village wept, the hamlets round
Crowded the consecrated ground;
And waited there to see the end
Of Pastor, Teacher, Father, Friend.

A TENTH OF EVERYTHING

IN the eighteenth century, pottery 'tithe babies' were popular. This four-figure group depicted a parson, a farmer and his wife and their baby: they are paying their tithes in kind. On the ground are their offerings: a pig; a sheaf of corn; and a basket of eggs. The farmer's wife is offering the parson her tenth child.

THE PARSON'S LOT

THE rector or vicar was decidedly unpopular while the reaping was going on, since on every tenth stook of corn a green branch was laid and those stooks belonged to the parson. So the reapers would sing showing their hatred not only of the tithe but of the parson who collected it.

Dryden introduced a harvest-home song into his play *King Arthur* or *The British Worthy*, 1691.

> We have cheated the parson, we'll cheat him again,
> For why should a blockhead have one in ten?
>> One in ten,
>> One in ten;
> For why should a blockhead have one in ten,
> For prating so long, like a book-learned sot,
> Till pudding and dumpling burn to pot?
>> Burn to pot.

It was a practice in the West Country during the fourteenth century onwards, for farmers to refuse to pay their dues to the parson until the parson had given a harvest feast and a pair of gloves to the workmen.

GET YOUR PRIORITIES RIGHT

IN Somerset and Dorset at Easter, the parish clerk used to carry round and leave at the house of each leading parishioner a packet of Easter cakes, thin and wafery and not unlike those used in the Jewish Passover rite. The clerk gave one cake for each member of the family and he was tipped in a like proportion. There was once a clerk who, receiving 5s. in return for five cakes said: 'Five shillings is handsome for the clerk, sir, but the Vicar only takes gold.'

CAUSE AND EFFECT

GOOD wine makes good blood, good blood causeth good humours, good humours causeth good thoughts, good

thoughts bring forth good works, good works carry a
man to Heaven; ergo good wine carrieth a man to
Heaven.

J. Howell

Professor David Knowles, in *Religious Orders in England*
(vol. II, p. 20), writes of:

the universal practice of breaking the great silence by
social drinking after Compline: when the Office was over
the night was yet young; some of the obedientaries had
been out all day and would not in any case rise for
Matins: this and the reluctance common to all ages and
callings to leave the warm precincts of cheerful day, led
to gatherings which were at best irregular, and usually
ended in excess, caballing and slackness in attendance at
office.

CONNIVANCE AND CONCUBINES

WE have in England a particular bashfulness in every-
thing that regards religion.

Joseph Addison

The clergy in the Middle Ages were forbidden by canons
to marry. Nevertheless, they did marry, though their
wives were called concubines. The married clergy, con-
cubinary priests, were subjected in their own persons, and
in the excommunication of their wives, to severe penalties;
these, however, were easily evaded, and their conduct was
connived at by judges often in the same predicament as
themselves. The prevalent connivance of the archdeacons
can be inferred from the fact that an oath was imposed on
them and on rural deans, that they would not take money

88

for tolerating the clergy to marry. This would hardly have been necessary if their connivance were not purchasable.

Hook, *Lives of the Archbishop of Canterbury*,
vol. III, 1865

NAUGHTY NUNS

IF you become a nun, dear,
   A friar I will be.
In any cell you run, dear,
   Pray, look behind for me.

James Henry Leigh Hunt, 'The Nun'

The custom of double monasteries was introduced into Britain from France. A lady of rank would surround herself with a sisterhood, and establish a nunnery. She had to make provision for the religious instruction of her tenants so a church was erected, and to serve the church, clergy and monks were required. They lived together and became Coenobites; the convents for the men and the women being under the direction of the lady of the manor, who constituted herself the abbess. Most of these establishments were abodes of religion and virtue, but they became liable to abuse and corruption.

In some of the nunneries the lady abbess would appear in a scarlet tunic, with full skirts and wide sleeves and hood, over an under-vest of fine linen of a violet colour. Her face was painted with stibium, her hair was curled with irons over the forehead and temples; ornaments of gold encircled her neck, bracelets were seen on her arms, and rings with precious stones on her fingers, the nails of which were pared to a point, to resemble the talons of a falcon. The shoes were of red leather. In the stricter convents, a more sober dress was adopted; but this was the dress of ladies of fashion, the *flammeae puellae* as they were called by Lullus; and such we are informed some of the abbesses remained. These vanities, on the part of both men and women, imply the existence of much social intercourse, and Alcuin complained of 'secret junketings and furtive compotations'; abbesses were warned that there should be not any dark corners in their houses, as advantages were taken of them for mischief.

ECCLESIASTICAL SNACKS

ARCHDEACON BURNE in his book *The Monks of Chester* records, in describing a monk's day:

Vespers was sung at five, followed by supper. After supper there was a reading in the chapter house called a collation, which was accompanied on the days when there was no supper by a little bread and beer or wine as a sort of night-cap. It is interesting to see how the name collation, which comes from a Latin word meaning 'bringing together' has got transferred in course of time from the reading to the night-cap, and now means a meal, especially a cold one.

TRENDY MONASTICS

EVEN monks in the early days were inclined to be up to date where fashion was concerned, a remarkable feat since cowl and cassock formed the basic uniform. The prologue to the *Canterbury Tales* gives some indication of monastic high living, mentioning the monk who went abroad to hunt and inspect farms, cutting a very elegant figure.

This monk was therefore a good man to horse:

Greyhounds he had, as swift as birds, to course.
Hunting a hare or riding at a fence
Was all his fun, he spared for no expense.
I saw his sleeves were garnished at the hand
With fine grey fur, the finest in the land,
And when his hood was fastened at the chin
He had a wrought-gold cunningly fashioned pin;
Into a lover's knot it seemed to pass.

Geoffrey Chaucer: *The Canterbury Tales* (*The Prologue*)
translated by Nevill Coghill, Penguin Books Ltd.

HAIR DISTINCTION

IN the Middle Ages all clerics were directed to follow the law laid down by the Constitutions of Cardinal Ottoboni. This law applied to dress—it was not to be so long or so short as to be an object of ridicule or remark. The cassock or clerical coat in length was to be well above the ankle, and the hair was to be cut so that it could not be parted and showed the ears plainly. In this way, by their corona and tonsure, and by the exterior form of their dress, they might be clearly known and distinguished from laymen.

ARCHIDIACONAL COIFFURE

DURING the first four centuries the clergy did not assume any peculiarity of appearance, except when engaged in the offices of the Church, as the adoption of a distinguishing habit would have marked them for persecution. One of the customs against which a certain proportion of the clergy preached, was the wearing of long hair by the men, a custom prevalent among northern nations, but denounced as encouraging effeminacy and vanity. Those who preached against the long locks of the laity were soon distinguished from the laity by clipping their hair. In the East, to shave the head was a ceremony expressive of affliction. The clergy of the Eastern Church shaved the front part of the head, leaving the hair on the back untouched, and to this custom the British clergy adhered. The Italians on the other hand, shaved their heads to what they termed the tonsure of St Peter: this consisted of a circle of hair round the shorn head, called a coronal tonsure since it was supposed to represent the crown of thorns.

The superintendence of this aspect of the clerical toilet devolved not on the barber but on the archdeacon.

'Clerks that wear long hair are to be clipped by the archdeacon, even against their will.' Archbishop Richard's Canons, 1175.

A BARBER'S PARADISE

WHEN the custom of wearing wigs came into fashion, the parson adopted it, in spite of the fact that the Early Fathers of the church thought wigs to be the invention of the devil, and that women who wore them were guilty of mortal sin. Charles II condemned the custom along with the 'sins' of smoking and reading sermons. The fashion, however, became widespread and even the shape of the surplice was altered with an opening down the front, to enable the parson to drape it around his shoulders instead of putting his head through the hole at the top.

In *Free Advice to a young Clergyman*, 1765, John Chubbe

advised the young preacher to wear a wig, till age made his own hair respectable. This custom persisted, certainly until 1858, when Archbishop Sumner wore a wig at the marriage of the Princess Royal of England.

CONFIRMATION OF A WIG

'ADDITIONS of other people's hair are entirely to be rejected, and it is a most sacrilegious thing for spurious hair to shade the head, covering the skull with dead locks. For on whom does the Presbyter lay his hand? Whom does he bless? Not the woman decked out, but another's hair, and through them another head. And if "the man is head of the woman, and God of the man," how is it not impious that they should fall into double sins? For they deceive the men by the excessive quantity of their hair; and shame the Lord as far as in them lies, by adorning themselves meretriciously, in order to dissemble the truth. And they defame the head, which is truly beautiful.'

Clement of Alexandria, *Stromata*

A RAG OF THE WHORE OF BABYLON

IT was the custom for the parson during divine service to wear a surplice. This particular garment was particularly disliked by the Puritans, who denounced it as 'a fool's coat', 'a habit of the priests of Isis'. It was this innocent garment which caused the 'Surplice Riots' which disrupted the calm of the city of Exeter when Dr Coleridge, vicar of Thoverton was mobbed. Francis Courtenay, vicar of St Sidwell's was attacked, it is said, by a yelling crowd of two thousand who covered him with filth and rotten eggs. *The Times* of that

day defended the conduct of the mob and asked the bishop
to put down the 'boyish nonsense' of the young clergyman
wearing a surplice.

> A very pretty public stir
> Is making down at Exeter,
>   About the surplice fashion;
> And many bitter words and rude
> Are interchanged about the feud,
>   And much unchristian passion.
>
> For me, I neither know nor care,
> Whether a parson ought to wear
>   A black dress, or a white one,
> Plagued with a trouble of my own,
> A wife who preaches in her gown,
>   And lectures in her night one.

Thomas Hood

HUNTING PARSONS

IT is not lawful for a bishop, or deacon to have dogs for
hunting or hawks!'

Council of Orleans

The Revd John Russell, perpetual curate of Swymbridge
in the West Country, was one of the last of the 'hunting
clerics'. As was the custom, Russell kept a pack of hounds
and the story is told that a Bishop of Exeter requested him to
cease doing so:

'Mr Russell, I hear you have a pack of hounds, is it
true?'

'It is. I won't deny it, my Lord.'

'Well, Mr Russell, it seems to me rather unsuitable for a clergyman to keep a pack. I do not ask you to give up hunting, for I know it would not be possible for you to exist without *that*. But will you, to oblige me, give up the pack?'

'Do y' ask it as a personal favour, my Lord?'

'Yes, Mr Russell, as a personal favour.'

'Very well, then, my Lord, I will.'

'Thank you, thank you.' The Bishop held out his hand. 'Give me your hand, Mr Russell, you are—you really are a good fellow.'

Russell gave his hand to the Bishop, who pressed it warmly only to hear the curate say: 'I won't deceive you—not for the world, my Lord. I'll give up the pack sure enough—but Mrs Russell will keep it instead of me!'

TO SMOKE A 'KEMBLE PIPE'

JOHN KEMBLE, a priest in the Diocese of Hereford, was arrested in 1679 when he was nearly an octogenarian, and accused of complicity in the Popish Plot. He was tried and sentenced to death by hanging and beheading. On the day of his execution Mr Digby the under-sheriff, took the reverend gentleman to the place of execution. He asked for time to say his prayers and have a last pipe of tobacco. Mr Digby agreed and joined him in his smoke. Kemble finished his pipe first, but Mr Digby had not finished his, so Kemble was asked to be good enough to wait until he had done so before going to his death. A last smoke in Herefordshire became known as 'a Kemble pipe'.

CATHOLIC PROTESTANT-CROUCH

As monks became old, certain concessions were made when

they attended services. As periods of standing were some-what prolonged seats in the choir were fashioned so that they could be tipped up and on the the underside was a small ledge on which the good monk could rest his pos-terior, retaining a semi-standing position. This concession was termed a 'misericordia' or 'act of mercy'.

It is thought by some that because these misericords came into contact with the posterior, the carvings on them were never of a sacred kind.

PARSON TOBY

THE old Derby toby jug representing a beer-drinking parson shows him wearing a long black clerical coat, with white bands and white stockings, and a cocked hat. The bands were a make-shift for the fine white linen tie edged with lace which parsons wore in the previous age. The nearest headgear we have to the parson's cocked hat in our day is the radar-like attachments on the hats worn occasionally by bishops and archdeacons.

PARSON BAITING

There wor a man in our town,
I knowed him well, 'twor Passon Brown,
A man of credit and renown
    For—he wor our Passon.

Passon he had got a sheep,
Merry Christmas he would keep;
Decent Passon he—and cheap,
    Well-spoke—and not a cross 'un.

Us had gotten nort to eat,
So us stole the Passon's sheep—
Merry Christmas us would keep;
    We ate 'n for our dinner.

Us enjoyed our Christmas day;
Passon preached, and said, 'Let's pray,
But I'm a fasting saint; aye, aye!
    You'm each a wicked sinner.'

Cruel vex'd wor Passon Brown,
Sick to death he laid him down,
Passonless was soon our town,
    For why?—we'd starved our Passon.

Tell'y—did'y ever hear
Such a story, true but queer,
How 'twixt Christmas and New Year
    The flock had ate their Passon?'

Old West of England Ballad

7

The Church Militant
and Recumbent

MIXED MOTIVES

IN olden days, reverence in the House of God was often quite lax, and so we find rhymes such as the following which have been preserved from bygone years:

> Some go to church to fetch a walk,
> Some go to church to have a talk,
> Some go to church to meet a friend,
> Some go there an hour to spend,
> Some go there to hear the news,
> Some go there to speak in pews,
> And yet, 'tis very strange and odd
> How few go there to worship God.

In certain parts of the country this rhyme ends in a different way:

> Some go there to see a lover,
> Some go there their faults to cover,
> Some go there to doze and nod,
> But few go there to worship God.

Pepys records: '1667, 26th May, the Lord's Day. I went by water to Westminster to the parish church, and there did entertain myself with my perspective glass up and down the church, by which I had the great pleasure of seeing and gazing at a great many fine women; and what with that, and sleeping, I passed away the time till the sermon was done.'

CHRISTIANS AWAKE

THE method by which people were kept awake in church was termed 'Bobbing'. The bobber walked along the aisles during service time, carrying a long stick like a fishing rod, which had a bob fastened to the end of it. When the bobber caught any person sleeping or talking they were given a nudge, usually on the head.

In some parishes the long wand had a nob on one end,

for men and boys, and a fox's brush at the other, with which the bobber tickled the noses of the fair sex who happened to be found dozing.

It is recorded that in Fleet parish church in Lincolnshire the practice of 'Bobbing' had fallen into disuse, but a former rector told the sexton that he wished to revive the custom, and even provided him with a new instrument for the purpose. The sexton was reluctant to resume his old duties saying:

'Well, sir, but be I to waken all of 'em?
Be I to nope Mr M—— on the head if I catches him asleep?' (alluding to one of the principal gentry in the parish).
'Well, Mike,' said the Rector, 'perhaps not Mr M—— nor Mr W——, nor Mr ——; but if you see anyone else sleeping rouse him up.'

By will, dated 17th April 1725, John Rudge gave 20s. a year, payable at 5s. a quarter, to a poor man, to go about the parish church at Trysull, Staffordshire, during sermon time, to keep people awake and to keep dogs out of the church.

HEAVENLY BELLS

THERE is an amusing account of a custom observed at Kerry Church in Montgomeryshire, for waking up sleepers during divine service. This was recorded in Bishop Thirlwall's 'Letters':

As I returned through the churchyard I was greeted very respectfully by a person whose dress seemed to indicate that he was a functionary of the church. I learned that he was the sexton but that he also discharged another very useful office, which, as far as I know, is peculiar to Kerry. It appears that it is by ancient custom a part of his duty to perambulate the church during service-time with a bell in his hand, to look carefully into every pew, and where ever he finds anyone dozing to ring the bell. He discharges this duty, it is said, with great vigilance, intrepidity and impartiality, and consequently with the happiest effect on the congregation; for, as everybody is certain, that if he or she gives way to drowziness, the fact will be forthwith made known through the whole church by a peal which will direct all eyes to the sleeper, the fear of such a visitation is almost always sufficient to keep everyone on the alert.

BUT ME NO BUTS

THE *Sporting Magazine* for July 1880, records that a clergyman of a Welsh church had a tame goat which attended divine service, and if it saw a member of the congregation drowsing, accepted it as a challenge, and launched so effectual a butt at the offender that he slept no more while the service lasted.

HIGGLEDY-PIGGLEDY

A FASCINATING entry in the records of Prestwich, near Manchester, for 1736 states: 'Thirteen shillings a year be given to George Grimshaw, of Rooden Lane, for ye time being; and a new coat (not exceeding twenty shillings) every other year, for his trouble and pains in wakening sleepers in ye church, whipping out dogs, keeping children quiet and orderly and keeping ye pulpit and churchwalks clean.'

A curious record is preserved in the 'History of the Church of Chester-le-Street', 10th August, 1834. 'In the middle of the morning service Joseph Lewin's ass passed through the church, and in the afternoon a hen and chickens. Both occurred in time of Divine Service.'

'FLAPPING THE CHURCH'

DURING the early part of the nineteenth century there was a custom in certain parts of the North of England called 'flapping the church'. Each young lad in the parish having furnished himself with a cord, to which was attached a piece of leather about six inches long, marched to church, led by the parish clerk. The church was lighted up for the occasion, the clerk shouting, 'Now, boys, flap away!' The boys beat all the pews in the church, both inside and out, and then turned their leather flappers on each other. The ceremony ended with a general steeplechase through the church when both pews and lads got a good dusting.

HAIR PARTING BY A THREE-LEGGED STOOL

WHEN Latimer was consecrated Bishop of Worcester in 1535, he expressed his disapproval of the introduction of pews into churches. At this time the aged and infirm used portable stools, and this appears to have been the practice for many years. The story of Jenny Geddes hurling her stool at the head of the Dean when Charles 1, at the instigation of Archbishop Laud, introduced the new service-book into Scotland, indicates that, even in 1636, fixed seats had not become general in the North.

Two families, the family of Baron Owen and the family of Nannau, dominated the Dolgelley area of Merionethshire and a bitterly waged feud continued between them well into the eighteenth century. A source of offence to the Owen faction was the existence in the parish church of a family pew of the Nanneys, so placed as to give the latter precedence. One day some of the Owen supporters broke into the church and hacked the pew to pieces. On the following Sunday the Owen supporters arrived at the church early and when the pew owners arrived they found the enemy in possession of the wreck, breathing defiance and armed to the teeth with pistols and daggers, ready to fight for the splinters.

HATS IN CHURCH

'At my devotion, I love to use the civility of my knee, my hat, and hand.'

Sir Thomas Browne

Even before the reign of Charles I, it was the custom to wear hats in church.

Samuel Pepys in his 'Diary' under 28th September 1662 (Lord's Day) records:

To the French Church at the Savoy, and there they have the Common Prayer-Book read in French, and which I never saw before, the Minister do preach with his hat off, I suppose in further conformity with our church.

And under 22nd September 1664 he writes:

Home to bed; having got a strange cold in my head,

by flinging off my hat at dinner, and sitting with the wind in my neck.

In Lord Clarendon's Essay on the decay of respect paid to age, he says that in his younger days he never kept his hat on before those older than himself except at dinner.

Alexander Barclay in his *Ship of Fools*, published in 1509, records a lack of reverence almost unbelievable in these days.

And when our Lorde is consecrate in forme of breade,
Thereby walks a nave, his bonet on his head.

SIGNS OF A PILGRIM

'MY sceptre for a palmer's walking staff'

Richard II, III. iii

The sign that a man was on pilgrimage in olden days was a wide brimmed hat and a rough cloak. He carried a staff with a hook on it to carry his bundle, or scrip, or purse. His beard and hair were allowed to grow. After return from the Holy Land he was entitled to wear a piece of palm in his hat, giving rise to the name 'palmer'.

WORSHIP OR ELSE

A RECORD exists in an old churchwarden's book of Great Faringdon, Berkshire, dated 1518, giving the form of admitting churchwardens at that period:

Cherchzewardenz thys shell be your charge to be true to God and to the Cherche for love nor favor of no man wythin this paroche to withold any ryght to the Churche but to reserve the dettye to hyt belongythe or ellys to goo to the Devell.

One of the churchwardens' duties was to watch over the spiritual and moral welfare of the parishioners and to ascertain that there was some valid excuse for any person being absent from Divine Service on a Sunday.

Towards the end of the eighteenth century it was the custom at Manchester, for the chief magistrate of the town, attended by the churchwardens and the police, to go out of the church while the first lesson was being read, and to compel all persons found in the streets to 'come into the church or pay a fee', which was fixed at 1s. for the lower classes and 2s. 6d. for those of higher rank.

KISS THE HAND THAT FEEDS YOUR SOUL

A CUSTOM of the pre-Reformation Church was that at the end of the Mass in which the whole congregation took part, a loaf of bread, called the 'Holy Loaf', or 'Holy Bread', was carried into the Chancel, and after being blessed by the priest, was broken up into small pieces and distributed to the people by the celebrant whose hand they kissed. This custom continued until the religious changes in the reign of Edward VI, but there were many agitators who wished to reinstate this custom long after it had ceased.

THOU SHALT NOT—ON SUNDAY

MR WARNER gives the following stanza, copied *verbatim et literatim*, from the stile which led to the village cemetery at Llanfair Iscoed, Monmouthshire:

> Who Ever hear on Sunday
> Will practis playing at Ball
> It may be before Monday
> The Devil will have you all.

In the registers of Holy Trinity, Chester, the following, sadly ironic, entry calls to mind an old custom.

> 1614 John Brookes Mason who poynted the steeple 1610 and made many showes and pastymes on the steeple of Trinity and also on the toppe of St Peter's Steeple as many thousands did witnesse, died 10 July and bur 11 July in the Church Yard broke his neck going downe a payre of Stayres by the Church.

Acrobatic feats on steeples, especially sliding down ropes extended from their summits, were not infrequent in bygone days. Both Edward VI and Philip were welcomed on entering London by rope dancers' descents from the battlements of St Paul's. Among other steeples similarly used may be mentioned those of Salisbury Cathedral, All Saints, Derby, and St Mary's, Shrewsbury.

PRIMITIVE LEARNING METHOD

In the old days, boys were flogged at the boundaries of the parish with the object of impressing them upon the boys' memories. The Chelsea churchwardens accounts show:

> 1670 Spent at the Preambulation Dinner . . 3. 10. 0.
> Given to the Boys that were whipt. . . . . 0. 4. 0.
> Paid for poynts for the Boys . . . . 0. 2. 0.

The custom of bumping boys against the stones and trees which mark the boundaries still persists in some country parishes and may well account for the practice of 'bumping' children on their birthdays.

CASTING OUT THE DEVIL BY BEELZEBUB

MANY customs among churchgoing folk have long since ceased to be remembered. One such was the congregational practice of spitting at the name of the devil, as if in contempt. Whenever Judas was mentioned, the members of the congregation expressed their abhorrence by smiting their breasts.

EYEWASH

WHERE a parish was situated near a Ffynnon Fair, the well of our Lady, or any other Saint, the water for baptism was always brought from it, and when the ceremony was over, old women would wash their eyes in the water from the font.

PIN WORSHIP

THE dropping of objects into holy wells was a relatively common custom. A crooked pin seems to have been used more than any other object. It was believed that if the pin was dropped with fervent faith, all the many pins which had been thrown into the well would be seen rising from the bottom to meet the new one.

GOD'S OLD PENNY

'GOD's penny' indicated the measure to which religion entered into the everyday life of the common people. It was a custom similar to the gift of the 'King's shilling' to a recruit on enlistment. It was not so much a partial or symbolic payment of the price as a first option. If the person receiving the penny were of a religious persuasion the penny was given to the church; if not, it was regarded as 'luck money'.

WHAT MANCHESTER DOES TODAY ENGLAND DOES TWO HUNDRED YEARS LATER

IN 725 a tax called 'Peter's Pence' was imposed on the people of Manchester by Ina, King of the West Saxons. It is not clear whether this was a forerunner of the tax called 'Peter's Pence' which was imposed by the Pope in the tenth century, or purely a local method of obtaining revenue.

KNOCK ONCE AND ASK FOR SANCTUARY

DURING the Middle Ages a hunted criminal was safe as soon as he clung to the sanctuary knocker. In Durham Cathedral there was a chamber above the door, where the monks kept constant watch. If sanctuary was claimed, the door was opened, the criminal's confession heard, the Galilee bell was rung, and he was offered the protection of St Cuthbert. The sanctuary knocker was clung to by murderers, horse thieves, debtors and prison breakers. At Durham between 1464 and 1525, 283 of those claiming sanctuary were murderers.

ECCLESIASTICAL BULL

IN certain parishes a charge was levied on the parson for keeping a bull for the use of his parishioners. It appears that this custom came to an end with the enclosure of the common fields and commons.

SHOES AND SOCKS FROM A BAITED BULL

By his will, in May 1661, 'George Staverton gave a sum of £6 to buy a bull, which bull he gave to the poor of Wokingham town and parish, Berkshire, being baited, and the gift money, hide and offal to be sold and bestowed upon the poor children in stockings of the Welsh, and shoes.' This custom ceased in 1823.

ARE NOT TWO SPARROWS SOLD FOR A FARTHING?

'1780—It is hereby agreed that only 3d. per dozen shall for the future be paid for sparrows, that they shall be brought to the churchyard on Sundays, with their bodies whole and unbroken and be paid for there; and if any Churchwarden shall pay for heads only at any persons' houses they are to pay the same out of their pockets.'

Neston Churchwarden's Accounts (Neston, Wirral)

GOD IS A GOOD WORKER BUT HE LOVES TO BE HELPED

Old Basque Proverb

In addition to honey, bees produce wax needed for the candles used in Church services. In the Middle Ages it was believed that there was a divine blessing on bees, making obligatory the use of beeswax candles during Mass. It was believed that while Adam and Eve were sinning in the Garden of Eden, the bees were so busy working that they did not witness the fall and, when they discovered it, they alone of all created kind, fled horrified from the garden (i.e. they were not expelled but left of their own accord).

THE TRUTH IS ALWAYS GREEN[1]

Spanish proverb

HENRY GREENE, by his will, dated 22nd December 1679, gave to his sister Catherine *Greene*, during her life, all his lands in Melbourne and Newtown, and after her decease to others, in trust, upon condition that the said Catherine *Greene* should give four *green* waistcoats to four poor women every year; such four green waistcoats to be lined with *green* galloon lace, and to be delivered to the said poor women on or before 21st December yearly, that they might be worn on Christmas Day.

ASTRONOMICAL SIDE-EFFECTS

BRUNDISH REGISTER of Baptisms records for 1600:

The 26th daie of October was Baptised Thomas Colbye the sonne of Thomas Colbye, gent, and Annye ux' beinge borne the 13th daie of October the signe beinge in Taurus at the hower of 7 of the clock in the evening.

FAITH IS A GREAT LADY, AND GOOD WORKS ARE HER ATTENDANTS

BY his will, dated 28th November 1611, one Leonard Dare directed the wardens of the parish of South Pool, in Devonshire, on St John's Day, to buy, bring and lay on his tombstone threescore penny loaves of good and wholesome bread made of wheat, and then and there to distribute the same to the poor of that parish. (This practice was also to be carried out on Christmas Day, Lady Day and Michaelmas Day.)

[1] La verda es siempre verde.

8

Bells, Smells and Yells

GET IT ON THE TABLE

By Wolsie's Gift
I measure time
For all ~ ~
To mirth, to grief
To church I serve to call[1]

There was a curious custom common in many parts of tolling the bell as the morning congregation left the church after service. One explanation, which has much to commend it, is that the bell was rung to warn the stay-away-house-wives and cooks to get the Sunday dinner on the table.

BELL ADVERTISING

THE one-time mine host of the 'Rosemary Branch', in South London, used to help his business thrive by sending the bellman around the district to announce the news that a fresh barrel of beer had been tapped.

DEATH TOLLS

YET the first bringer of unwelcome news
Hath but a losing office, and his tongue

[1] Inscription on the bell 'Great Tom' given to Sherborne Abbey in 1502.

Sounds ever after as a sullen bell,
Remember'd knolling a departed friend.

Henry IV, Part 2, 1, i

In the twelfth century Durandus wrote: 'When anyone is dying, bells must be tolled that the people may put up their prayers—twice for a woman and thrice for a man; if for an ecclesiastic, as many times as he had orders.'

Men's death I tell by doleful knell;
Lightning and thunder I break asunder;
On Sabbath all to church I call;
The sleepy head I raise from bed;
The winds so fierce I do disperse;
Men's cruel rage I do assuage.

THIRSTING AFTER RINGING

ALE for the refreshment of the ringers was a worthy custom in olden days. On occasions the belfry became known as a tippling place and special jugs were employed to carry ale from the local inn. Some of these 'ringers' jugs' still remain and many of them were capable of holding between sixteen and twenty quarts of ale. They were usually inscribed with the names of the ringers and these lines:

If you love me doe not lend me,
Euse me often, and keep me clenly,
Fill me up or not at all,
If it be strong, and not with small.

'THE CURFEW TOLLS THE KNELL OF PARTING DAY'

Thomas Gray

WILLIAM THE CONQUEROR made a law that at the

ringing of a bell, called the 'couvre feu' (cover fire) at eight o'clock all people should put out their lights and fires and go to bed. This law was an attempt to prevent fires breaking out in the wooden hovels, which then comprised the towns and villages.

'REMEMBER, REMEMBER'

IN the parish of Harlington, Middlesex, in 1683, half an acre of land was given apparently for the benefit of the bell-ringers of the parish, to provide them with a leg of pork, for ringing on 5th November.

NORTHAMPTON BELL-LANGUAGE

You owe me a shilling,
Say the bells of Great Billing.
When will you pay me?
Say the bells of Middleton Cheney.
When I am able,
Say the bells of Dunstable.
That will never be,
Say the bells of Coventry.
O, yes, it will,
Says Northampton Great Bell.
White bread and sop,
Say the bells of Kingsthorpe.
Trundle a lantern,
Say the bells of Northampton.
Roast-beef and marsh-mallows,
Say the bells of All Hallows.
Pancakes and fritters,
Say the bells of St Peters.
Roast-beef and boiled,

Say the bells of St Giles.
Poker and tongs,
Say the bells of St Johns (hospital).
Shovel, tongs and poker,
Say the bells of St (Se)pulchres.

GREAT CALL

PULL on, brave boys, I'm metal to the backbone,
I'll be hanged before I'll crack.

From a Norfolk village tower

The 'ring' of 12 bells at St Paul's was heard for the first
time on All Saints Day, 1878. They were cast by John
Taylor & Co of Loughborough and Sir Edmund Beckett
claimed them to be 'on the whole unquestionably the
grandest ringing peal in England and therefore in the
world'. The heaviest bell of the ring, 'Great Paul', 16 tons,
14 cwt, 2 qrs, with the note of E flat, has a motto chosen by
Canon Liddon. Under the arms of the Dean and Chapter is
inscribed, *Vae mihi si non evangelizavero*. In St Paul's Epistle
the words meant, 'Woe is me if I preach not the Gospel'.
Canon Liddon, translating on behalf of the bell, put it this
way, 'May I be cracked if I don't call people to church'.

SWINGING IDENTIFICATION

BELL makers were proud of their craftsmanship, and loved
to adorn their bells with decorative designs and marks by
which the founders could be identified. Thomas Ballisdon,
of London, who supplied many bells in the early sixteenth
century, used the mark of a hanging bell and the initials T.
and B. on each side.

It was a common custom to dedicate bells to saints and

while bells are treated as feminine in the craft, almost every saint in the calendar is duly honoured in some bell inscription and dedication.

From time to time bell makers have immortalised their own names upon their work, and inscriptions such as, 'Hew Watts made me 1563', are not uncommon. Occasionally a bell that has been recast praises the skill of its new founder at the expense of its first maker. A bell made by Alexander Rigby at Stamford, Lincolnshire, went to Badgeworth in Goucestershire, where it seems not to have given satisfaction. It was recast by Abel Rudhall of Goucester, who caused the following to be inscribed on it:

> Badgeworth ringers they are mad,
> Because Rigbe made me bad;
> But Abel Rudhall you may see
> Hath made me better than Rigbe.

ECCLESIASTICAL PESTICIDE

PROBABLY the strangest use to which bells have been put was that of cursing, 'by bell, book and candle'. A wood-cut of a silver bell made by Benvenuto Cellini for Pope Clement VII is given in Chambers's *Book of Days*. It bore a rich display of carvings on the exterior representing flies, grass-hoppers, other insects and serpents, the purpose of the bell having been to serve in a Papal cursing of these creatures when they became so troublesome as to demand that method of castigation.

FOR WHOM THE BELL TOLLS

IN 1705 a sum of money was left to the parish of St Sepulchre, London, to pay the sexton to toll the bell prior to every execution at Newgate. Noorthouch, in his *History of London*, says that the sexton

comes at midnight, and after tolling the bell calls aloud:

'You prisoners that are within
Who for wickedness and sin,

after many mercies shown to you, are now appointed to die tomorrow in the forenoon, give ear and understand, that tomorrow morning the greatest bell of St Sepulchre's shall toll for you in form and manner of a passing bell, as used to be tolled for those that are at the point of death; to the end that all goodly people hearing that bell, and knowing it is for your going to your deaths, may be stirred up heartily to pray to God to bestow his grace and mercy upon you whilst you live.'

On the morning of execution, as the condemned criminals pass by St Sepulchre's churchyard to Tyburn, he tolls his bell again, and, the cart stopping, he adds, 'All good people pray heartily unto God for these poor sinners who are now going to their death, for whom this great bell doth toll. Ye that are condemned to die, repent with lamentable tears; ask mercy of the Lord for the salvation of your own souls, through the merits, death and passion of Jesus Christ, who now sits at the right hand of God, to make intercession for as many of you as penitently return unto him

Lord have mercy upon you!
Christ have mercy upon you!
Lord have mercy upon you!
Christ have mercy upon you!

ANY OLD IRON

DURING the reign of Edward VI the destruction of church

property was enormous and bells were not excluded. The bells were broken up, and the metal was exported in large quantities or sold at home to be converted into cannon.

Sir Henry Spelman records that 'in the year of our Lord 1541, Arthur Bulkley, Bishop of Bangor, sacrilegiously sold five fair bells belonging to his cathedral, and went to the seaside to see them shipped away; but at that instant was stricken blind, and so continued to the day of his death'.

NATURE'S DEODORANTS

In the Elizabethan period the pews of the nobility were frequently decorated with flowers, and quite often pews were 'strawed' with primroses, cowslips, violets, marjoram and marigolds. This custom was not followed for purely decorative purposes. Erasmus visited London in the time of Henry VIII, and described the floors of palaces, even those of royalty, as strewed with rushes to camouflage their dirt.

ARCHIEPISCOPAL SEWAGE DISPOSAL

Archbishop Matthew Parker, 1559–75, made at Lambeth Palace 'conveyances underground to cleanse and keep his house sweet, by sinks to carry away filth into the Thames. This cost him no small amount of money, but it tended much to the health of his family. These drains were of brick, arched, and so high that a man might easily walk upright in them.'

Ducarel

COVERED ALL OVER WITH SWEET VIOLETS

There was a custom unique to Naseby in the last century

an old description of which is worth quoting. 'There are walls in some of the houses said to be two hundred years old built of clay, and were they drawn over with lime-mortar and marked or lined to appear as stone-work, their appearance would be respectable.' One vicar of the parish thought they were by no means respectable; for, 'instead of this, the new coat which they have once a year consists of cow-dung, spread upon them to dry for firing'. This coat was then scraped off before the winter and used to be stacked up in front of the houses to be used as fuel.

THERE'S NO PLACE LIKE HOME

DURING the tenth century, houses, even in the towns, were only thatched huts. A wooden platter and a drinking horn or two were the utensils of an ordinary home. Mead was the chief drink, and this, as well as wine, was taken to excess. Nothing can give us a better idea of the rough custom of the time, than the account which has been handed down to us of King Edmund's death.

He was giving a feast at Pucklechurch, in Gloucestershire, when a man, upon whom the king himself had passed sentence of outlawry, after an exile of six years, returned, and not only took his place at the royal table, but actually seated himself close to the king. The king motioned to the cup-bearer to remove the intruder, who resisted. Upon this, the king rushed upon him, seized him by the hair and dashed him to the ground. The outlaw meantime had drawn his dagger and plunged it into Edmund's breast, who immediately expired. The assassin was cut in pieces by the royal guards.

Hook

THE village festival called the Wake was a time when men could prove their manhood and the lasses could use the festivities for husband-hunting. What young man could resist the maid who won 'The Grinning Match through a Collar', when the prize was a piece of fat bacon—'(no crab-apples to be used)'.

And what maid's heart did not flutter over the farm lad's antics in the competition advertised thus:

A YOUNG PIG

will be turned out, with his ears and tail well soaped, and the first person catching and holding him by either, will be entitled to the same.

Bull-baiting, dandy races, apple dumpling eating and bear baiting all added to the excitement, which, together with the ale consumed, usually ended in fisticuffs. H. Cottom recorded how one, Joseph, from Flixton, at one Eccles Wake,

had fought several times, and in honour of his victories was far advanced in drunkenness. A wag told him that a person was ready to fight him and that everybody said Joseph was afraid to tackle him. Annoyed at this, Joseph said that he had thrashed several that day and was quite ready to thrash another. They told him that he would find his opponent, who was no other than the bear, in the inn stable. Joseph went into the stable and his companions shut the door. He stumbled over the bear, who immediately grabbed him, and in spite of Joseph's well-directed blows, almost squeezed that worthy to death. He managed to get out of the bear's clutches at last, and made for the door. When he got out, his friends asked him how he got on. 'By th' mass, lads,' said he, 'he's too strong in't arms for me, but only let th' devil take his top coat off and I'll give him what for.'

The poet Drayton wrote, after visiting the Lancashire Wake:

So blyth and bonny now the Lads and Lasses are,
That ever as anon the Bag-pipe up doth blow,
Cast in a gallant Round about the Harth they goe,
And at each pause they kisse, was never seen such rule,
In any place but here, at Boon-fire, or at Yeule;
And every village smokes at Wakes with lusty cheere,
Then Hey the cry for Lun, and Hey for Lancashire.

BEAR EVENSONG

WHEN, in the early nineteenth century, a bear arrived in a certain village in Lancashire on Wakes day, the service of Evensong was only half completed in the parish church. This, however, was rapidly terminated by the parish clerk calling to the preacher from the west door, 'Minister, th' bear's come; and what's more there's two of 'em'. Such freedom of speech in a holy place is more easily understood when it is realised that the rector and his family and personal friends usually watched the bear-baiting from the church-yard adjoining the village green.

SPORTSMAN

'No man is fit to be called a sportsman wot doesn't kick his wife out of bed on a haverage once in three weeks!'
Robert Smith Surtees

Any occasion for celebration, be it fair, wedding or whatever, was also an occasion for indulgence in sport, a popular form of which was the ancient game of quintain. This consisted of an upright post with a crossbeam turning on a pin. At one end of the revolving crossbeam was a board, at the other a heavy sandbag. The aim of the game was for the player to ride against the board and strike it with a lance, and it required great skill and dexterity to pass by before the sandbag, swinging round, struck the player from his mount, subjecting him to the yells and jeers of the onlookers.

PUNISHMENT BY GARBAGE DISPOSAL

The pillory at Manchester in the early nineteenth century was erected in the market place when it was needed. It was supported on a platform raised about ten feet off the ground on a post. The offender was made to stand on the platform with his head and hands securely clamped in the wooden cross-piece for a prescribed time while onlookers pelted him with rotten eggs and other unsavoury missiles.

'THOU SHALT NOT SUFFER A WITCH TO LIVE'

Exodus 22.18

In the year 1541 Cranmer instructed the clergy 'to seek for any that use charms, sorcery, enchantments, witchcraft, soothsaying, or any like craft of the devil.'

The punishment for witchcraft was death as is evident from the register of St Andrew's, Newcastle.

August 21, 1650: 'These partis her under named were

executed on the town mor for wiches. Isabell Brown for a wich.'

The names of fourteen others classed as witches follow. The punishment may seem somewhat barbaric but it must be remembered that up to the end of the seventeenth century people were believed to die from the effects of being bewitched.

TRIAL BY BIBLE

'ONE Susanah Hannokes, an elderly woman of Wingrove, near Aylesbury, was accused by her neighbour of bewitching her spinning wheel, so that she could not make it go round, and offered to make oath of it before a magistrate; on which the husband, to justify his wife, insisted upon her being tried by the church Bible, and that the accuser should be present. Accordingly she was conducted to the Parish Church, where she was stripped of all her clothes to her shift and undercoat, and weighed against the Bible; when, to the no small mortification of her accuser, she outweighed it, and was honourably acquitted of the charge.'

Gentleman's Magazine, 1759

THE JUDGEMENT OF THE GLOWING IRON

ALL punishment is mischief: all punishment in itself is evil.

Jeremy Bentham

Criminals in the last resort could appeal to be judged of God. This was a distinctly religious ceremony in ancient times and the whole of the proceedings were in the hands of the clergy. The judgement of the Glowing Iron was one form of this trial. The iron was placed before the altar from where the priest, clad in full canonicals with the exception of the cope, removed it with a pair of tongs to the fire, where it was heated during the celebration of Mass. It was then sprinkled with Holy Water when the following prayer was recited: 'The Blessing of God the Father, the Son and the Holy Ghost, descend upon this iron for the discerning of the right judgement of God.' The accused was then required to carry the iron in his bare hand a measured distance—nine feet divided into three equal parts. His hand was then enclosed in an envelope under seal for three days when it was examined to see if it were foul or clean. If the wound had festered, the accused was judged to be guilty; if not, he stood acquitted. Other variants of this idea are as follows.

THE JUDGEMENT OF THE PLOUGH SHARES

THIS necessitated the accused person walking barefoot and blindfolded in a certain area where nine hot plough shares had been laid lengthwise at irregular intervals. It is alleged that this form of trial by ordeal was undertaken by Queen Emma, mother of Edward the Confessor, when it was believed she had committed adultery with Alwyn, Bishop of Winchester.

THE JUDGEMENT OF THE BOILING WATER

AFTER the priest had celebrated Mass and had chanted the Litany he exorcised and blessed the water which was to be boiled. He then stripped the accused of his clothes and dressed him in ecclesiastical vestments of the kind worn by a deacon. Prayers were said and after the accused had said the Lord's Prayer, the judge suspended a stone in the water, which the accused, in the name of God, had to draw out from the cauldron at the depth of his wrist or his elbow, according to the severity of the ordeal. On the third day his hand was inspected and his innocence or guilt determined.

'THE POWER OF PUNISHMENT IS TO SILENCE, NOT TO CONFUTE'

Samuel Johnson

THE ducking-stool had its origin in a Saxon superstition against cutting or maiming a woman's body. Thus, women who were found guilty of crimes punishable by death, were drowned. The ducking-stool is an inheritance of those times.

The *cucking stool*, *ducking stool*, and *tumbrel* have often been confused, and indeed most writers appear to consider them but different names for the same thing, but, as Mr Llewellyn Jewitt points out, they are all three distinct varieties of punishment. The cucking-stool is mentioned in Domesday Book as having been in use in Chester, and the name (*cathedra stercoris*) casts a light upon the degrading nature of its origin. In it the culprit, who might be of either sex, was placed, usually before his own door, to be pelted and insulted by the mob. On the tumbrel again he was drawn round the town or village, seated in the chair, which was sometimes so constructed as to be suitable also for ducking; but the ducking-stool par excellence was specially made for purposes of immersion.

About 1774 the ducking-stool in Manchester 'consisting of a chair on the end of a long lever extending over the water, was used for punishing "scolds" and prostitutes'. It was originally erected at Poolfold and later was moved to Daub-holes, the Infirmary pond at Piccadilly.

THE JUDGEMENT OF COLD WATER

In this judgement the accused was thrown into a pond or tank or pit. If he floated, he was adjudged guilty; if he sank, his innocence was regarded as divinely proved. Swimming was not allowed and to ensure that the person did not swim his thumbs were tied to his toes.

THE JUDGEMENT OF THE MORSEL

This was the test of eating consecrated bread and cheese. It was known as the Corsned, or Morsel of Execration. The priest wrote the Lord's Prayer on the bread and did likewise with the cheese. Under the right foot of the accused was set a Cross of poplar wood. Another Cross was held over the man's head. The charge was thrown over the head of the thief written on a tablet and the bread and cheese at that moment were placed in the mouth of the accused with prayers, included in which was this statement:

If thou wast a partner in this theft or didst know of it, or hadst any fault, that bread and cheese may not pass thy gullet and throat.

SKIN FOR SIN

In the olden days the punishment for robbing the churches consisted in flaying the offender and affixing his skin to the church door. This penalty for sacrilege appears to have had the sanction of the law in Anglo-Saxon times, when money was often paid by the offender to save his skin, called 'Hide Gold', a ransom for one's skin.

A bit of the skin of a murderer was often purchased as a charm: people believed that their house would never catch fire so long as this gruesome relic was present. The mutilation of bodies in chains was common in early times, and the hands and feet and hair of the dead were cut off. The hands were thought by thieves and robbers to enable them to open any lock and get into any house without being detected in their crime.

ROUGH JUSTICE

Tit for tat.
If you kill my dog
I'll kill your cat

Professor A. M. Low, records that justice, during the reign of Richard I, was rough and ready.

If a seaman should kill another on board ship he was bound to the dead body and thrown into the sea. If he killed another seaman on land he was bound to the dead man and the two buried 'quick' together.

9

Death Aids

SAY IT WITH FLOWERS

THE practice of using flowers at funerals has its origin in antiquity; not only did they smell sweet to disguise the odour of the corpse but they were also regarded as protectives against infection. When the plague was at its height, Dekker in *Wonderful Yeare*, 1603, records that rosemary, which could normally be bought at the price of twelve pence an armful, rose to six shillings a handful.

The traditional funeral emblematic flowers and trees are:

Oak—signifying virtue and majesty

Ivy—immortality

Passion flower—the crucifixion

White lily—futurity

Palm—martyrdom

Rosemary—remembrance

Cypress—symbol of life and reproduction also of infernal deities

Rosemary was regarded by ancient and classical authorities as the most highly esteemed among flowers because it was believed to retard putrefaction.

PILGRIMAGE OF PETALS

COMMON to most nations and peoples is the custom of visiting the graves of loved ones with offerings of flowers.

This is well recorded in epitaph. The best known was once in Loughor churchyard, in Glamorgan:

> The village maidens to her grave shall bring
> Selected garlands each returning spring—
> Selected sweets—in emblem of the maid
> Who underneath this hallow'd turf is laid;
> Like her they flourish, beauteous to the eye;
> Like her, too soon, they languish, fade, and die.

ROSES FOR LOVERS

IT was recorded by Bishop Gibson (in his edition of Camden's *Britannia*) that in Surrey, a custom existed whereby rose trees were planted on graves, especially of young men and women who had lost their lovers. This custom was common among the Romans and the Greeks.

THE VIRGIN'S CROWN

A QUAINT Hampshire funeral ceremony was that of 'carrying the Virgin's crown'. The crown, from which fine paper gloves hung, was made of thin wood, covered with paper and decorated with black and white rosettes. It was carried in front of the coffin from the house of the deceased to the church by two young girls attired in white dresses, white shawls and white hoods, with a white wand between them to which the crown was attached. During the service the crown was placed on the coffin by one of the girls, and at the close it was again suspended from the wand and borne to the grave.

Words of Mrs Hemans, inscribed as an epitaph at Bathampton, recorded this custom:

Bring flowers, pale flowers, o'er the grave to shed,

A crown for the brow of the early dead;
Though they smile in vain for what once was ours,
They are Love's last gift—bring flowers, pale flowers.

EVERLASTING TOKENS

At the funeral of an unmarried girl, garlands were placed on the coffin and afterwards they were hung in the church over the seat which she had occupied. These garlands were made either with flowers or with paper rosettes and the coffin bearers on such an occasion were young maidens. In certain counties paper cut-outs of gloves or handkerchiefs were also suspended from the garland. In the parish of Llandovery the garlands and gloves used to hang in the church for a year and were taken down on each anniversary of the death of the virgin. The virgin's grave was decorated with flowers, and a pair of gloves was laid on it. These gloves were taken away by the nearest relative who visited the grave on that day. It was the custom for the nobility, and especially soldiers of high rank, to have their armour hung up in church following their burial. So we have parts of some churches nearly filled with armour, helmets, pikes, lances and other weapons.

PRAYERFUL FLORA

In some places it was customary for the friends of the dead to kneel and say the Lord's Prayer over the grave for several Sundays after the interment, and then to dress the grave with flowers:

> Manibus date lilia plenis.
> Purpureos spargam flores; animamque nepotis
> His saltèm accumulem donis, et fungar inani
> Munere.

Bring fragrant flowers, the fairest lilies bring,
With all the purple beauties of the spring.
These gifts at least, these honours I'll bestow
On the dear youth, to please his shade below.

Warton

SIN EATING

PRIOR to a funeral, it was customary, when the corpse was brought out of the house and laid upon the bier, for the next of kin, widow, mother, sister or daughter (for it had to be a female), to give over the coffin, a quantity of white loaves, in a green dish, and sometimes a cheese, with a piece of money stuck in it, to certain poor persons. After that they presented, in the same manner, a cup of liquid and required a person to drink a little of it immediately.

When that was done they knelt down and the minister, if present, said the Lord's Prayer, after which, they proceeded with the corpse. At every cross-road between the house and the church, they laid down the bier, knelt and again repeated the Lord's Prayer; and did the same when they first entered the churchyard. It was also customary in many places to sing psalms on the way to the grave.

CARRYING THE COFFIN

THIS is our master, famous, calm and dead,
Borne on our shoulders.

Robert Browning, 'A Grammarian's Funeral'

The bier was usually carried by the next of kin; a custom considered to be the highest respect that filial piety could pay to the deceased. Thomas Pennant points out that this was a frequent custom among the Romans of high rank.

It was thought a great continuance of the good fortune which had attended Metellus Macedonicus through his whole being, that when he had, in the fulness of years, passed out of life by a gentle decay, amidst the kisses and embraces of his nearest connections, he was carried to the funeral pile on the shoulders of his four sons.

To this day it is regarded as a great honour to be chosen to be a bearer, and this office in time past was performed by children and relatives of the deceased.

The present-day practice of carrying the coffin shoulder high is comparatively recent. In generations past, long lengths of strong linen were passed under the coffin and the bearers wrapped the ends round the forearm enabling them to a carry a heavy weight with comparative ease.

DAMP DEPARTURE

AMONG Welsh people in past generations it was regarded as a mark of great fortune on the deceased if it should rain while he was being carried to the grave, that his coffin might be wet with the dew of heaven.

BUMPING THE CORPSE

'THE Lamentation of a Sinner' was to be found at the end of the Metrical Psalms in most old Prayer Books. As the corpse was being carried to the graveyard it was 'bumped' three times, or carried round the graveyard three times and the Lamentation of a Sinner was sung. The first and last stanzas were:

> O Lord, turn not thy face away
> From him that lies prostrate;

> Lamenting sore his sinful life,
>   Before thy mercy's gate.

and the last,

> Mercy, good Lord, mercy I ask,
>   This is the total sum;
> For mercy, Lord, is all my suit,
>   O let Thy mercy come.

FUNERAL BELLMAN

OUR Church, in imitation of the saints of former ages, calls on the minister and others who are at hand to assist their brother in his last extremity. In order to do this she directs that when anyone is passing out of this life a bell be tolled . . .

(Wheatley's commentary on the *Book of Common Prayer*)

One of the parish officials in medieval times was the bellman. The bells he used seem to have been the property of the parish. They were called 'Rogation Bells', because of their use in calling people to the church, and they were rung in the funeral procession from the house of the deceased parishioner to the church.

At Oxford it was the custom for a bellman to precede the funeral procession of any member of the university and this custom also prevailed in certain parts of Wales, the bell being carried about the streets and rung just before the interment of a corpse. Such a bell is generally known as the 'Lyche bell', or 'Corpse bell'.

In 1463, John Baret of Bury St Edmunds, directs that the two bellmen, who go about the town on his death announcing his funeral, are to have gowns given to them. 'And at my "Yeer Day", he adds, they are to have each

4d. for going about the town to call on the inhabitants "to pray for my soul, and for my faderis and modrys", and the same for ringing on the "Months Mind".'

HURDY-GURDY INTROIT

YET another custom in the middle of the fifteenth century was the use of a chime barrel set with the tune of the *Requiem Aeternam*, the Introit of the Mass for the dead. This Introit ranged over five notes only, and the instrument was wheeled through the town grinding out this lament for some departed inhabitant.

EXIT BY CANDLELIGHT

IN 1780 it was the custom for the inhabitants of the town of Poulton to be buried by candlelight. It was regarded as a sacred duty to expose a lighted candle in the window of every house as the corpse passed through the streets towards the church for interment.

RESURRECTION AIDS

ANCIENT practices demanded that mourners had to carry branches of yew and throw them into the grave after the body had been committed. It was thought that they would shoot and they were thus regarded as symbolic of the resurrection of the body, as well as the immortality of the soul. In Wales bay leaves were strewed before the corpse.

CAKE AND ALE SEND OFF

WHEN the Danes occupied England, a solemn feast was always given after the funeral of a king or noble by his successor. This was called the 'arfwol'—from 'arf', meaning inheritance, and 'wol', meaning ale—a word signifying that the feast was given by the heir on succeeding to an estate through a death.

Hence we find surviving in rural parts of the country, arval-cake and arval-ale, partaken by mourners after a funeral.

EAT AND PRAY

DR ROCK tells us in 'Church of our Fathers', that after a death, Placebo, or Evensong of the Dead, was sung overnight, and the Dirge, or Matins of the Dead (followed usually by two Masses) in the early morning. Then, after breakfast, the Solemn Mass or Requiem was sung and there was the offering of the Mass-Penny by the friends, after which they went to the burial and thence to the funeral dinner.

DEATH ASSURANCE

THE practice of 'waking' or 'watching' beside a body was really to make absolutely sure that the person was dead and not in a coma. In the process of time, like many other praiseworthy customs, this practice was used as an occasion for excessive drinking and festivity.

A FOOLS' PARADISE

IN olden days a village funeral hardly ever took place without the presence of the parochial idiot. Sir Walter Scott depicts this aspect in *Guy Mannering*—

And then 'the funeral pomp set forth,' says he, 'saulies with their batons and gamphions of tarnished white crape. Six starved horses, themselves the very emblem of mortality, well cloaked and plumed, lugging along the

136

hearse, with its dismal emblazonry, crept in slow state towards the place of interment, preceded by Jamie Duff, an idiot, who, with weepers and cravat made of white paper, attended on every funeral, and followed by six mourning coaches filled with the company.'

It was the free feast which generally proved the attraction. A funeral was considered a poor affair if there was not a drunk to be seen.

GRIEF THERAPY

'HERE at Gloucester', says Walpole in his *Letters*, (1753) 'is a modernity which beats all antiquities for curiosity. Just by the high altar, is a small pew hung with green damask with curtains of the same, a small corner cupboard painted, carved and gilt for birds in one corner, and two troughs of a birdcage with seeds and water. It belongs to Mrs Cotton, who, having lost a favourite daughter, is convinced her soul is transmigrated into a robin redbreast, for which reason she passes her life in making an aviary of the Cathedral of Gloucester. The Chapter indulge this whim, as she contributes abundantly to glaze, whitewash and ornament the church.'

LASTING TESTIMONIAL TO POOR SERVICE

MOST epitaphs, particularly those belonging to the eighteenth and nineteenth centuries, carried plain words of warning to the living.

'Reader, prepare to meet thy God', threatens one in Berriew churchyard. Another, in Chester Cathedral, advises with sly wisdom, 'Wait awhile and you'll follow me'. An epitaph at Cross kirk, Northmarine, Shetland, however, was not simply plain, it was personal too; not to mention slanderous. Written of Donald Robertson, born 1st January 1785, died 4th June 1848, aged 63 years, it read:

> He was a peaceable quiet man, and to all appearance a sincere Christian. His death was very much regretted, which was caused by the stupidity of Laurence Tulloch, of Clotherton, who sold him nitre instead of Epsom Salts, by which he was killed in the space of 3 hours after taking a dose of it.

TALE OF THE OLD IRON POT

WE brought nothing into this world and we can carry nothing out—but some do the next best thing.

Along with the conventional head stones and crosses so usually found in churchyards, and the pieces of sculpture— anchors, angels, and broken pillars with mourning drapes— there are, occasionally, more unusual decorations. At Wood Ditton, near Newmarket, on a gravestone in which was fixed an iron dish, according to the instruction of the deceased, were these words written by him before his death:

> WILLIAM SYMONS ob. 1753 aet. 80
>
> Here lies my corpse, who was the man
> That loved a sop in the dripping pan;
> But now believe me I am dead
> See here the pan stands at my head.
> Still for sops till the last I cried,
> But could not eat, and so I died.
> My neighbours, they perhaps will laugh,
> When they do read my epitaph.

10

Final Departure

ANCIENT EUTHANASIA

In ancient folklore, history and myth are so intermingled that it is often difficult to get at the truth in any situation. From some of the earliest accounts of travellers in Britain it is known that the death of the aged by violence was a common element of the native customs. 'They die only when they have lived long enough; for when the aged men have made good shear and anointed their bodies with sweet ointments, they leap off a certain rock into the sea.'

Elton, in his *Origins of English History*, indicates that this was a custom in the North and it was certainly the way in which the ancient Swedes and Pomeranians killed their old people. It was the custom of many savage and primitive tribes to place the old people in large earthen jars with some food and leave them to perish. There is evidence of this in ancient India. In other primitive civilisations when people became so old as to be unable to perform the least office for themselves, they were placed in a solitary hut at a distance from the family group with a small stock of provisions within their reach. Here they were left to die of hunger or be devoured by the wild beasts. In ancient folklore the instrument of violent death that looms largest is the mallet. We have recorded the practice of Norsemen throwing themselves off the cliff but if the old person became too frail to travel to the cliff in order to throw himself over, his kinsmen would save him the disgrace of dying 'like a cow in the straw', and would beat him to death with the family club.

Elton's *Origins of English History* cites an old English country story of 'The Holy Mawle', which 'hung behind the church door, which, when the father was seaventie the soone might fetch to knock his father on the head, as effoete, and of no more use.'

Ancient folklore and traditions point to instances in England and Wales where sons pulled their fathers out of bed and killed them to save the disgrace of their dying in bed (Nutt, *Legend of the Holy Grail*).

The old custom of the barbarous use of the mallet in killing the aged and infirm died out but there are still records of such instruments coming to light with inscriptions such as:

> Who to his children gives his bread
> And there by himself suffers need
> With this mallet strike him dead.

> Here is the fair mall
> To give a knock on the skull
> To the man who keeps no gear for himself,
> But gives all to his bairns.

DREAM OF THE DEAD AND YOU'LL GET NEWS OF THE LIVING

In the early days of the Christian Church in Britain it was not unusual to bury high-ranking persons in the church porch and it is perhaps not mere coincidence that ancient documents record that young people used to sit and watch in the church porch on St Mark's Eve, from 11 at night until 1 a.m. This experience having been suffered three years running, in the third year it was believed that those keeping vigil would see the ghosts of all those about to die in the coming year passing into the church.

James Montgomery in his 'Vigil of St Mark' describes it thus:

'Tis now, replied the village belle,
St Mark's mysterious Eve;
And all that old traditions tell
I tremblingly believe.

How, when the midnight signal tolls
Along the churchyard green,
A mournful train of sentenced souls,
In winding-sheets are seen.

The ghosts of all whom death shall doom
Within the coming year,
In pale procession walk the gloom,
Amid the silence drear.

DEATH PREDICTIONS

THERE were curious customs attached to the times when death occurred. In some parishes it was believed that if a death occurred on New Year's Day it would be followed by one in each month of the year. In other parishes it was believed that if a corpse remained unburied over the Sunday another death would occur in the parish within the month.

There is an ancient Manx custom which relates that cottagers used to look for the traces of a footmark in the ashes of the grate. If the toes appeared to point towards the door it was thought a death would occur, if towards the fireplace, a birth.

It was believed that when a candle wick curled upon itself it represented the handle of a coffin. The person at whom it pointed at the time was believed to be in danger of death.

A HELPING HAND

IN some parts of the country sick people were placed on the floor for their last hours of life. It was believed that a person could not die easy on a bed made of the feathers of wild birds.

It was also thought that sweepings from the floor by the altar, brought to the bed of a dying person, would shorten a lingering death. Yet another custom to help a person die easier was to place a paten containing salt on the breast of the dying person.

An idea which lingers in remote country areas even now is that opening all the windows and undoing all the locks in the home will assist the passing of the soul from the body in death.

There was also the belief that the quicker the dead person's spirit left the room the less chance there was of its being captured by evil spirits.

TRANSPORTATION FEE

THE custom of placing two coins upon the eyelids of a corpse is believed to have originated in ancient Greece and Rome where a coin was placed in the mouth of the corpse before burial to pay the fee of Charon, the ferryman of mythology who transported the souls of the dead over the rivers of the nether regions on their way to judgement.

STING OF DEATH MUST BE SHARED

RATHER a quaint custom was that of 'Telling the Bees'. When someone died in a family which owned beehives, the nearest relative to the deceased person had to go as soon as possible to the hives and knock on each one and announce aloud the fact of the death in the house. It was believed that if this was neglected the bees would desert the hive, never to return.

'YN GARN Y BO TI'

THERE is an ancient custom recorded in 2 Samuel, 18.17 —'And they took Absalom and cast him into a great pit in the wood, and laid a very great heap of stones upon him.' Travellers as they went by this spot used to throw a stone to add to the heap, signifying their loathing of their own rebellion as Absalom had rebelled against David his father.

'Yn Garn y bo ti', was a Welsh curse. 'May such villains be buried under a heap of stones.' Villains were often buried at the crossroads and travellers often threw stones over such graves muttering the curse. Until 1823, the bodies of suicides were directed to be buried at crossroads, with a stake driven through the body.

The Parish Registers of Ledbury record:

AD 1605 Nell Biggor an aged pson was cast into a pit in the brooke the viith day of May.

AD 1593 Thos. Barker being an excommunicat pson was put into a grave out of Christian burial and was not buried the viith day of April.

A STONY END

A STRANGE custom seems to have prevailed in certain parts

of Anglesey centuries ago. Bodies were buried close to the surface, with a layer of lime over the corpse. This was not very unusual in itself, for the period and the rocky ground might well have necessitated shallow graves. The unusual feature of these interments was the presence of a small round white stone on the chest of the deceased. It may be that this custom refers to 'To him that overcometh will I give . . . a white stone, and in the stone a new name written, which no man knoweth saving he that receiveth it '(Revelation 2.17).

CHRISTIAN DISPOSAL

THE land round about the church was called the cemetery from the word Coemeterium 'a dormitory', it being in the Christian sense a sleeping place of the dead who had died in the Lord. It was also called the 'Churchyard', or even, 'God's Acre'.

From very early times attempts were made to put a stop to the practice of holding fairs in the cemetery and to prevent anything being sold in the porches of churches. By the Synod of Exeter, in 1267, Bishop Quevil ordered that all the cemeteries in his diocese should be enclosed securely and that no animal was to be allowed pasturage on the grass that grew in them. The Bishop directed that: 'All church cemeteries must be guarded from all defilement, both because they are Holy (in themselves) and because they are made Holy by the relics of the Saints.'

The reason for this belief in the holy character of cemeteries is set out clearly in a letter of Bishop Edyndon in 1348, where he says that 'The Catholic Church spread all over the world believes in the resurrection of the bodies of the dead. These have been sanctified by the reception of the Sacraments and are consequently buried, not in profane places, but in specially enclosed and consecrated cemeteries, or in churches, where with due reverence they are kept, like the relics of the Saints, till the Day of Resurrection.'

The sacred character of consecrated cemeteries was recognised by the law. Bracton says that 'They are free and absolute from all subjection, as a sacred thing; it is only amongst the goods of God—whatever is dedicated and consecrated to God with Rights and by the Pontiffs, never to return afterward to any private uses.' And amongst these he names 'Cemeteries dedicated, whether the dead are buried therein or not, because if those places have once been dedicated and consecrated to God, they ought not to be converted again to human uses.' Indeed, 'Even if the dead are buried there without the place having been dedicated or consecrated, it will still be a sacred place.'

The ceremony by which the medieval churchyard was consecrated was carried out by the bishop of the diocese, or some other bishop with his authority. The fees were to be paid by the parish. Parochial accounts give illustrations of this expense being borne by the churchwardens. At Yatton, in 1486, the churchyard was enlarged and the bishop came to consecrate the ground. The parish entertained him and his assistants at dinner and paid the episcopal fee which was thirty-three shillings and fourpence. One of the expenses on this occasion was noted by the wardens thus: 'We paid the old friar that was come to sing for the parish, 8d.'

GRAVEYARD PROTECTION FOR THE LIVING

LLANELLTYD churchyard in Merionethshire is circular and

has probably been in use for over 1300 years. T. P. Ellis, writing in 1928, claimed that in olden times the altar in a church was regarded as a very holy place since people believed that on the altar Christ was, in the strictest literal sense of the word, actually present. That being so, anyone who claimed the protection of the altar, no matter what he had done, could not be touched. He was at once protected by the altar and by God from the vengeance of men, and round the sacred altar a circle was drawn, within which a man, so long as he remained within that circle, could claim sanctuary for seven years and seven days.

It appears that the limits of the circle were determined by a ploughman standing at the foot of the altar with his arm outstretched and, in his outstretched hand he held the yoke of his plough team. A plough team consisted of eight oxen yoked two abreast, and the yoke extended from the front of the first couple to the end of the plough. Holding the yoke in his hand, the ploughman swept it round in a circle, and all the land within that circle, which was called the 'erw', became holy ground. That is the origin of the phrase 'God's Acre', for 'erw' means acre. It was the immediate circle of God's protection, not of the dead, but of the living, however guilty.

T. P. Ellis, *Dogelly and Llanelltyd*

WRONG SIDE OF THE SHROUD

A SECTION of the churchyard was sometimes left unconsecrated for the purpose of burying excommunicated persons. In Southwark, there was at one time a burial ground termed 'The Single Woman's Churchyard', which was reserved for the burial of the inmates of the licensed stews who were usually excommunicated.

The north side of the churchyard became known as 'the wrong side of the church'. So in the register of Hart, Durham, there occurs the following entry:

Dec. 17, 1596, Ellen Thompson Fornicatrix (and then excommunicated) was buried of ye people, in ye chaer at ye entrance unto ye yeate or stile of ye churchyard, on the east thereof.

GRAVEYARD WEAPONS

SEVERAL reasons have been given for yew trees in churchyards. The most likely are that their poisonous foliage keep animals away from the area, and their wood, being ideal for bows, kept the villagers' constant needs supplied.

In Shakespeare's *Richard II*, Scroop says to the King:

> The very beadsmen learn to bend their bows
> Of double-fatal yew against thy state;
>
> Act III.ii

GRAVE CLOTHES

> No mask like open truth to cover lies,
> As to go naked is the best disguise.
>
> William Congreve

The Burial Service in the *Book of Common Prayer* is so worded as to assume that no coffin is used. Reference is always to the 'body' or 'corpse'. 'When they come to the grave, while the corpse is made ready to be laid into the earth . . . .'

In 1710 Wheatley wrote of, 'When the body is stripped of all its grave clothes, and is just going to be put into the grave etc.'.

The Prayer Book also instructs that 'earth shall be cast upon the body', not on the coffin.

In the reign of Queen Elizabeth, it was the custom to bury merely in a winding sheet, without a coffin.

PROMOTION OF THE WOOLLEN TRADE

KING JAMES II issued an order through his Privy Council that everyone should be buried in a woollen shroud, in order to promote trade.

Thus, following the Burial in Woollen Act it was the practice at the conclusion of the Burial Service at the grave for the parish clerk to call out, 'Who makes Affidavit?'

'We, Frances Norris and Anne Stonnaxe, of the Hamlet of Westwick, do make oath, that Matthew Lynton, of Westwick, buried 13 Oct. 1678, was not put in, wrapt up, or wound up or buried, in any shirt, shift, sheet, or shroud, made or mingled with flax, hemp, silk, hair, gold or silver, or other than what is made of sheep's wool only; nor in any coffin lined or faced with any cloth, stuff, or any other thing whats', made or mingled with flax, hemp, silk, hair, gold or silver, or any other material but sheeps wool only.

Dated 18 Oct. 1678
Thos. Buck.'

The Register Book of the Parish of Dolgelley in the County of Merioneth, provided by virtue of the Act of Parliament for burying in 'woolen', covers the period 1678 to 1708, and the entries of burial are supported by two affidavits that the corpse was buried in 'woolen' only, and the affidavits are attested by the Rector.

UPPER-CLASS CUSTOMS DIE HARD

THE upper classes objected strongly to the Burial in Woollen Act and did what they could to evade the law. Pope wrote of Mrs Oldfield, who was buried in Westminster Abbey in a Brussels lace headdress, a holland shift with tucker, and double ruffles of the same lace, and a pair of new kid gloves, these words:

'Odious! in woollen! t'would a saint provoke!'
(Were the last words that poor Narcissa spoke);
'No, let a charming chintz and Brussels lace
Wrap my cold limbs, and shade my lifeless face.'

TWO SIZES ONLY

WITH the uncoffined dead, it was simple to discover whether the Burial in Woollen Act had been complied with. Up to the end of the seventeenth century it was quite common to bury bodies without coffins, simply wrapped in wool, so that the body mingled freely with the common earth. In olden times it was usual for the parish to provide a coffin for general use, which was known as the 'Parish Coffin'. In most parishes two coffins were kept, a large one and a small one. The Burial in Woollen Act was sometimes evaded by covering the corpses with hay or flowers which were known as 'strewings'.

ARRESTED BURIAL

IT was once a general belief that a corpse could be arrested for debt. The last attempt to carry out this illegal practice was, according to J. C. Cox, as late as 16th October 1811.

Two seventeenth century register references to this practice are:

1659 (Alstonfield, Staffs), Aug. 30. Humphrey Dakin, buried about 2 of the clock in the night, fearing an arrest.

1689 (Sparsholt, Bucks). The corpse of John Matthews of Fawler, was stopt on the churchway for debt August 27. And having laine there fower days, was by justices warrant buryed in the place to prevent annoyances—but about six weeks after it was by an Order of Sessions taken up and buried in the churchyard by the wife of the deceased.

OLD-FASHIONED DEODORANT

PLAGUE swept England during the reign of James the First. The worst outbreak was in 1625. It brought trade to a standstill, and in London, streets were deserted and men were afraid to meet each other. It is recorded that there were 'near 1,000 deaths a day'. Funerals were so close together that '3,000 mourners went as if trooping together, with wormwood and rue stuffed in their ears and nostrils'.

NO ROOM IN THE CHURCHYARD

THE plague was called the posting sweat, 'that posted from towne to towne throughe England, and was named "stope gallant" for hytt spared none, for ther were dawncyng in the cowrte at 9 o'clocke that were deadd or eleven o'clock'.

The greatest number of deaths occurred in the months of August and September 1665. Ten thousand were estimated to have taken place in one week. Records at this time were in a state of chaos but it is said that the parish of Stepney lost, within the year, 116 sextons, grave-diggers and their assistants. The churchyards became full and large pits had to be dug to which the dead from the plague were carried in cartloads, collected by the ringing of a bell and the cry of 'Bring out your dead'. It is estimated that the plague carried off 100,000 people in London alone.

During the plague, a field given over to burial became known locally as 'Dead man's Field'.

A TOKEN OF LASTING LOVE

BURIAL of the heart in a separate place was a custom limited in the main to the twelfth and thirteenth centuries, although instances of it have been recorded before and since.

1583 Captain Thomas Hodges:
At Wedmore is a monument sacred to the memory of Captain Thomas Hodges of the County of Somerset, esq., who at the siege of Antwerpe, about 1583, with unconquered courage wonne two ensignes from the enemy, where receiving his last wound, he gave three legacies: his soule to his Lord Jesus, his body to be lodged in Flemish earth, his heart to be sent to his dear wife in England.

Here lies his wounded heart, for whome
One kingdom was to small a roome:
Two kingdoms therefore have thought good to part
So stout a body and so brave a heart.

PERISHABLE GOODS

WHEN Hugh de Grentemaisnil died, some monks salted up his body, enclosed it in a hide, and sent it to Normandy. (He was a Norman baron, who had distinguished himself in the Battle of Hastings and was granted the manor at Charlton, about eight miles from Oxford, in 1081.)

Edward Jesse, *An Angler's Rambles*, 1834

In time past when it was desired to remove a body a

great distance for burial, it was necessary to remove its internal organs, which were usually buried where the person died.

Norton, Durham:
March 22 1756 bur: the heart and bowells of the right honourable James Earl of Wemyss. The remains was buried with his Ancestors at Weyms Castle in Scotland, the 8th day of April.

GRAVEYARD JOHN THE BAPTIST

THERE was an old superstition that the first corpse to be buried in a new churchyard was always seized by the devil. In many parishes where a new churchyard was acquired, the locals would refuse to have their loved ones buried there until at least one body had been laid to rest. It usually happened that a stranger or a servant of a visitor who died in the parish 'went before' the locals.

A DEATH FALLACY

THERE was a popular belief in olden days in certain counties, certainly in Cheshire and Glamorganshire, that the road along which the corpse had been taken to the parish grave-yard became a public highway. This is, of course, false.

ROBBED BY ROBING

IN the olden days it was the practice that if a corpse was carried for burial to a distant church through several parishes the executor had to pay fees for burial and for tolling of the bell in each parish. It was the custom for the bell to be rung and the vicar to be robed in each parish to insure the payment.

AND THE DEVIL TAKES THE HINDMOST

LICHGATES were usually small structures built in either wood or stone forming an archway over the path leading into the churchyard. There was an old superstition that the spirit of the last person buried in the churchyard watches over the churchyard till another person is buried, to whom he delivers his charge. This custom tended to lead to some unseemly scenes in many churchyards, especially when two burials were to take place on one day. There is a record of a certain day in the county of Argyll when two burials were to take place in one churchyard.

Both parties staggered forth as fast as possible to consign their respective friends in the first place to the dust. If they met at the gate, the dead were thrown down till the living decided by blows whose ghost should be condemned to portery.

Sir John Sinclair, *Statistical Account of Scotland*

It was also believed that it was unlucky for a wedding procession to meet a funeral procession entering the churchyard. To prevent such an encounter some churches arranged access to the churchyards by different routes. This arrangement used to prevail at Barthomley church in Cheshire, where it was believed that misfortune, if not death within the year, would befall a bridal pair who passed through the Lichgates.

PROFESSIONAL PERKS

A CURIOUS custom is recorded in the registers of Tregaron Parish in Cardiganshire. In addition to the usual fees, the Parish Clerk received certain 'perks' in the case of a funeral.

At the death of every marryed man and woman there is —— to ye Clerk of ye man's wearing apparel, his best hat and his best shoes and stockings, and from every woman her head flannen or hood, her best shoes and stockings, beside what is due for digging of their graves.

At most funerals a 'Mortuary' was usually received in lieu of small tythes forgotten during a person's lifetime.

William Wade who died as a stranger, I, John Goffe, parson of Ripe, had his upper garment which was an old coate, and I received for the same 6s.

The burial offerings were not always the perks of the clergy; in some parts of the country, and especially in Wales, mourners were expected to put something 'on the plate' for the surviving relatives especially if they were poor.

FUNERAL EXTRAS

ANOTHER custom connected with burial fees had to do

with the use of the processional cross. Most parishes possessed a processional cross and also a cheaper cross which
was used at funerals, but occasionally on payment of an
extra fee, a more elaborate cross would be used. Parishes
which were lucky enough to have a rich processional cross
in terms of silver and jewels, used to rent it out to neighbouring parishes.

In the same way, the churchwardens seem to have hired
out the bier and the candlesticks to be used at funerals in
other parishes for the payment of a fee. The record of the
parish of Ashburton for 1523–24 notes that 'The best Cross
and parish tapers' were hired to a neighbouring parish for
a fee of 21s 8d.

During the Middle Ages parishioners also paid for the
use of the parish cross and candlesticks at funerals in their
own churches.

PAYMENT FOR PRIVILEGE

'BURIAL without a coffin, 1s; for a grave in the church,
6s. 8d.; in the chancel, 13s. 4d. But the most honourable
Grave of any man whatsoever is in the Churchyard, because
that shows most honour to God's house. The great first
Christian Emperor, Constantine, and many of his successors,
were buried in the Churchyard.'

The Register of Great and Little Abingdon

St Paul's Churchyard, Mousehole, Cornwall:

on DOLLY PENTREATH

Old Doll Pentreath, one hundred age and two,
Both born, and in Paul Parish buried too;
Not in the Church 'mongst People great and high
But in the Church-yard doth old Dolly lie!

THE tomb of Piers Shonkes, bears the inscription: 'Hoc Tamen in Muro Tutus'. This tomb is at Brent Pelham church, Hertfordshire, where the story goes that the devil swore he would have Piers Shonkes whether he was buried within the church or outside it. So to outwit the devil he was immured in the wall of the church so that his corpse lay neither inside nor outside.

There are many similar legends. Perhaps the most interesting is that connected with the tomb in the north wall of the church of Tremeichion in North Wales. The vicar, Daffydd Ddu, about 1340 is said to have made a bargain with the devil that the vicar should practise the black art with impunity during his life but that the devil should possess his body after death whether he was buried within, or outside the church. It is said that the vicar proved himself more than a match for the devil by arranging to be buried in the church wall.

MONEY-MAKING CORPSE

UNDER a flagstone which formed the entrance to the vaults of the old church of St Mary Matfelton, Whitechapel (long since replaced) were deposited the remains of Richard Parker, the hero of the mutiny at Nore. On 30th June 1697, he was executed at the yard-arm of the man-of-war *L'Espion*, and was buried in a common grave at Sheerness. Very soon after the burial, his widow employed some 'resurrection men', to steal the body from the grave. The corpse was afterwards discovered by an ancestor of Dean Champneys being publicly exhibited in the neighbourhood of Whitechapel. Through his concern the body was brought to the church and interred.

BLEEDING BODIES

> AN orphan's curse would drag to hell
> A spirit from on high:
> But oh, more horrible than that
> Is the curse in a dead man's eye!

There was an old superstition that the body of a murdered person bled afresh if approached by the person guilty of the murder. Thus the custom arose of murdered corpses being displayed in public. The bodies of Lords Warwick and Montacute lay in St Paul's in Easter week, 1471—'That all men might see them'.

On 22nd May 1471, the body of Henry v was exposed before the high altar of St Paul's for two days, 'Where he bled'.

GRAVE WARNINGS

'1720, buried Jane Cressop, who was killed by the colo-quintada or bitter apple, which she took to procure an abortion. God give others better grace.'

'Elizabeth Harper, who lived in Sidgate, rip open her owin belle with a par o' sesers; the wound was six inches long and her pudens cam out and lay on each sid of her, and was bur. 8 Aug. 1703.'

'1776, Catherine, wife of Richard Parrott, her second husband, by her own express orders, buried entirely in white, and her grave covered with flowers in the 70th year of her age.'

157

This gave rise to the saying in the parish of Clovelly,

> Under the Turf poor Kate is laid,
> Who married twice and died a maid.

TAKE HEED OF DRINK

IN the Registers of Croydon, under 1585,

'William Barber, a common drunkard and blasphemer, beinge dringinge tyll he was drunken, was found dead on the xixth day of September, he beinge soe he was layd in a grave, and not cov'rd tyll the xxijth day of the same month for the coroner to vew (and then cov'ed).'

'1673 April 23, was buried Mr. Thomas Sharrow, Clothworker, late Churchwarden of this parish, killed by an accidental fall in a vault, in London Wall, Amen Corner, by Paternoster Row, and was supposed had lain there eleven days and nights before anyone could tell where he was. Let all that read this take heed of drink.' (St. Benedict Fink, London)

ESCHEW

IN the Arlingham Register there is a burial entry under 1763.

Stephen Aldridge, who was suffocated by a flatfish, which he unadvisedly put betwixt his teeth when taken out of the net; but by a sudden spring it made into his throat and killed him in two minutes. It is here recorded as a warning to others, to prevent the like accident.

HERE LIES IN VERTICAL POSITION

THERE is the story of Ben Jonson to the effect that he is buried upright in his grave at Westminster Abbey.

158

The Dean of Westminster rallied the poet one day about his burial in the Abbey vaults. 'I am too poor for that', said Jonson, 'and no one will lay out funeral charges upon me. No sir; six foot by two wide is too much for me—two feet by two will do for what I want' 'You shall have it', replied the Dean.

> Besides, in the place They say there's no space
> To bury what wet-nurses call "a Babby."
> Even 'Rare Ben Jonson,' that famous wight,
> I am told, is interr'd there bolt upright,
> In just such a posture, beneath his bust,
> As Tray used to sit in to beg for a crust.
>
> *Ingoldsby Legends*

In the 'White Doe of Rylstone' by Wordsworth, reference is made, in the first canto, to erect burials:

> Pass, pass, who will, you chantry door,
> And through the chink in the fractured floor,
> Look down, and see a grisly sight,
> A vault where bodies are buried upright;
> There face to face, or hand to hand,
> The Claphams and Mauleverers stand.

There was a tradition that the bodies of the Claphams were buried upright in the vault of Bolton Priory church.

A RARE PRACTICE

ON 12th July 1868 a certain Madame Beswick was buried at Harpurhey cemetery. It is said that this lady had a terrible fear of being buried alive so she directed her body to be embalmed by her physician (Dr Charles White).

This mummy was for many years exhibited in the Natural History Museum, Peter Street, and when the museum was closed, the corpse of Madame Beswick was commited to the ground.

ALL AT SEA

'SAMUEL BALDWIN, Esquire, sojourner in this parish, was immersed without the Needles, sans cérémonie, May 20.'

Tradition has it that just before he died Samuel Baldwin expressed a desire to be buried at sea in order to frustrate his wife's frequently expressed threat, that if she survived him, out of contempt, she would dance on his grave.

NONE TOO SWEET SMELLING SAVOUR

ROSAMOND CLIFFORD, a rare beauty of her age, was concubine to King Henry II, who was said to have built a labyrinth at Woodstock to hide his mistress from his jealous Queen Eleanor.

Rosamond was buried in a nunnery at Godstow near Oxford, with this epitaph:

Hic jacet in tumulo Rosa mundi non Rosa munda;
Non redolet sed olet quae redolere solet.

This tomb doth inclose the world's fair rose, so sweet and full of favour;
And smell she doth now, but you may guess how, none of the sweetest savour.

Fuller records how

Her corpse may be have said to have done penances

160

after her death; for Hugh, Bishop of Lincoln, coming as a visitor to this nunnery, and seeing Rosamond's body lying in the quire under a silken hearse, with tapers continually burning about it, thought the hearse of a harlot, no proper object for eyes of virgins to contemplate on; therefore caused her bones to be scattered abroad. However, after his departure, those sisters gathered her bones together again, put them into a perfumed bag, and enclosed them in lead, where they continued until ousted again in the reign of King Henry the Eighth.

THE PARTING KISS

DEAN COMBER, Dean of Durham in 1691 wrote:

The ancient Christians were wont to give a parting kiss of charity to the body just when it was about to be put in the grave, to declare their affection, and to evidence that he died in the unity and peace of the Church, for which we still say, 'Our dear brother or sister', which pious custom is yet observed in the Greek Church, and also in the northern parts of England by the near relations, who usually come near and kiss the deceased before he be put in the grave.

There was a time when coffins were made with a hinged lid so that the relatives could see the body before it was committed to the ground. Sometimes a window was made in the lid for this purpose.

FAITH IN THE RESURRECTION

He that fears death, or mourns it, in the just,
Shows of the resurrection little trust

Jonson

It was the custom in some parishes that when a coffin was about to be placed in the grave, the nails securing the lid were drawn out. This was done for the convenience of the deceased at the day of Resurrection!

11

Seasonal Sauce

ADVENT IMAGES

As unhappy as the man that has not seen the Advent Images.

Old Yorkshire saying

In the North of England it was the custom during Advent to dress two dolls, one to represent the Saviour, another the Virgin Mary. These images were paraded around the houses and a halfpenny was asked for from the people who saw them. This became known as the 'Vessel Cup', and was associated with the good will song:

> God bless the master of this house,
>   The mistress also,
> And all the little children
>   That round the table go.

These dolls were surrounded by evergreen leaves, and everybody to whom the 'Advent Image' was shown was allowed to take a leaf. This was carefully kept as it was believed to be a remedy for toothache.

AN APPLE IS A BOY'S BEST FRIEND

On St Thomas' Day groups of boys would wander through the village or town singing:

> Wassail, wassail, through the town,
> If you've got any apples, throw them down;

Up with the stocking and down with the shoe,
If you've got no apples, money will do;
The jug is white and the ale is brown,
This is the best house in the town.

TRADER'S CHRISTMAS PRESENT

THERE used to be a custom of making at Christmas little
images of paste, called 'Yule-doughs', which were given by
bakers to their customers. Originally these images were
intended as representations of the child Jesus and the Virgin.
The 'Yule-doughs', however, have long since degenerated
into puddings and mince pies made simply to be eaten.

TREES OF DOUBTFUL KNOWLEDGE

IN parts of Montgomeryshire on Christmas Day it was the
custom when the sun came through the branches, to bless
the apple trees. Also on 17th January in some parts of the
country groups of wassailers used to visit the orchards of
cider-apple trees paying special attention to the newly
planted trees. The leading wassailer dipped a piece of burnt
toast into cider which was offered to him and lodged it in
the fork of the new tree. The aim was to enable it to bear
more fruit. (Anglo-Saxon word 'wes-hel' meaning 'to be
in health'.)
The wassailers would sing or intone the verse:

Old apple tree we wassail thee
    And hoping thou wilt bear;
For the Lord does know where we shall be
    To be merry another year.

To blow well and to bear well
    So merry let us be,

And every man drink up his cup
And health to the old apple tree.

Also:

Apples now, hatfulls, capfulls, three bushel bagfulls, tallets ole fulls, barn's floor-fulls, little heap under the stairs.

THREAT OF GOBLINS

An' the gobble-uns 'll git you
Ef you don't watch out!

James Whitcomb Riley

Down with the Rosemary and so
Down with the Baies and Mistletoe:
Down with the Holly, Ivie, all
Wherewith ye drest the Christmas Hall.

Herrick

Christmas decorations had to be taken down by Candlemas or, so the story went, the householder would see goblins.

TWELFTH NIGHT BEANO

The Epiphany or Twelfth Night was the time for choosing the Mock King. An Epiphany cake was made, into which was placed a ring, or a silver coin, or in the oldest tradition of all, a bean. The male getting the slice of cake containing the token was crowned King of the Bean, and ruled the company for a limited period. In some areas it was the custom to appoint a Queen also, chosen by a similar method through the Epiphany cake, the token in the Queen's case, however, being a thimble or a pea.

The bean was thought to possess magical qualities and

165

was certainly regarded as a symbol of the female principle. In France one could obtain sugar beans for the King's Cake; the outer layer was the shape of a bean; the second layer showed a baby's face showing through the split, the last layer of the sweet was in the shape of a child wrapped in swaddling clothes.

LONG-RANGE WEATHER FORECAST

ST PAUL'S DAY, which falls on 25th January, used to be very important for people living in the country since it provided them with what they believed was a long-range weather forecast.

The rhyme connected with this custom is as follows:

> If the Day of St Paule be cleare,
> there shall betide an happie year:
> If it do chance to snow or raine,
> then shall be deare all kinde of graine.
> But if the winde then bee alofte,
> warres shall vex this realm full oft:
> And if the cloudes make dark the skie,
> both neate and fowle this yeare shall die.

NIGHT OF BEER AND STONE-THROWING

IN some parts of Cornwall, it was the custom on the eve of the Conversion of St Paul (25th January) to throw stones at a pitcher, until it was shattered. On what was called 'Paul's Pitcher Day', jollification and drinking accompanied the stone pelting. It would seem that this custom had its origin in the commemoration of St Paul's part in the martyrdom of Stephen.

EARLY SOCCER BAN

FOOTBALL is spoken of in the fifteenth century and during the reign of James I, a rule was made to 'debarre from this court all rough and violent exercise as the football, meeter for laming than for making able the users thereof'. But children still played the game, in spite of the king's rule, and in Chester it was always played in the streets of the city on Shrove Tuesday.

HOME COOKING

AT St Ives in time past the children would tie stones to cords and walk around the town on Shrove Tuesday slinging the stones at the doors, yelling:

> Give me a pancake, now—now—now,
> Or I'll souse in your door with a row—tow—tow.

In other parts children would go from house to house begging sweetmeats and singing some version of the following rhyme:

> A-shroving, A-shroving!
> We be come a-shroving.
> A piece of your fat bacon, please,
> A pancake or a bit of cheese,
> All of your own making.

JACK O'LENT

AN ancient Ash Wednesday custom was the making of a Jack o'Lent. This figure was made of straw and was dressed up in old clothes. It was supposed to represent Judas, the disciple who betrayed our Lord with a kiss. This figure was carried through the streets on Ash Wednesday and then set up in order that people might throw stones and sticks at it during the season of Lent. At the end of Lent, the Jack o'Lent was publicly burnt.

In some parts of the country a Holly boy and an Ivy girl, roughly made figures, were burnt on Ash Wednesday. The Holly and Ivy plants are symbols of the male and female principles.

ANGELS LAUGH AT THE DEVIL ON HORSEBACK

DURING the Middle Ages the Lenten arrangements for feeding the monks and nuns from Ash Wednesday to Easter Sunday ensured that food did not interfere unduly with their devotions. Apart from a limited number of eggs, the staple food in Lent was salted and dried fish. Conger, bream, ling and codling stock fish, whiting and mackerel are among the fish named in Russell's *Book of Nurture*. The salt fish was prepared in a variety of ways and disguised with mustard sauce and other seasonings. It is not surprising that after six weeks of salt herring, stock fish and the like, the inhabitants of the cloisters looked forward to Easter Day and the ancient custom of 'The Devil on Horseback', —a split red-herring appearing to ride as a jockey on the back of a duck, prepared by the convent or monastic cook.

A page showing the expenses for Easter Week of the Grace Dieu nuns is as follows:

A stall-fed ox: 16s.
1 pig from the farm, 3 small pigs: price 14d.
1 calf: price 2s.
Almonds and raisons: 12d.
and for Friday, 150 fresh herrings and a stock fish, 2s.

A CAKE FOR MOTHERING SUNDAY

SOME people in the North of England believed that the simnel cake was named after an old couple, Simon and Nelly. These two, the story goes, were expecting the local children to come 'mothering' but there was nothing in the house to offer them. All that old Nelly had was a lump of lenten dough and the stale remains of the Christmas pudding. The couple used their ingenuity, and agreed to enclose the pudding in the dough but when it came to cooking the cake Sim, as his wife called him, wanted to boil it, whereas Nell felt baking would be best. So adamant were they both that blows were resorted to with broom, fists and stools. When they were both exhausted, a compromise was arrived at. The concoction was first boiled, then baked, using the wood from the broken broom and stool for fuel, and the eggs broken in the fisticuffs to glaze their creation. And the first Sim-Nell cake appeared on the Lenten scene.

It was an early French custom to impress simnel cakes with the figure of Christ or the Virgin Mary and they were known as *pain-demayn* or 'Bread of our Lord'. It is possible that the cakes originally carried a pagan mark and had their place in the pagan rites of the Teutonic races. This was the case with hot-cross buns, or Easter cakes, which the Saxons ate in honour of their goddess Eastre. The Christian leaders, unable to stamp out this custom, incorporated them into Christian celebrations by marking them with a cross.

SUNDAY NAMES

CHILDREN in the North, especially in Cumberland, used the following couplet to remember the Sundays from mid-Lent to Easter:

> Tid-Mid, Misera
> Carlings, Palms, Pace Egg Day.

The name 'Carling Sunday', for Passion Sunday, or the fifth Sunday in Lent derives from the custom of people having carling nuts, a kind of pea, fried in butter. A pancake was made of these and it was eaten with salt and pepper.

In the Midlands, Palm Sunday was known as 'Fig Sunday'. This custom may have had some connection with the cursing of the barren fig tree by Jesus. Even the poorest of people would contrive to get a handful of figs on Palm Sunday.

A PALMLESS SUBSTITUTE

FROM earliest times it was the custom in England on Palm Sunday that the priest should bless palm-twigs and distribute them to the people and that the people would then go in procession with the priest singing and shouting their Hosannas. The so-called 'Palms' in England were probably willow, box or yew, charges for which appear in the churchwardens' accounts. Some authorities claim that the reason yew trees are so frequently found in churchyards was in order to furnish the yew branches which usually served for palms on Palm Sunday.

CLEAN FEET, SORE HANDS

ON Maundy Thursday in most of the cathedral churches in the Middle Ages, and in the greater parish churches, the feet of 13 poor people were washed with great ceremony and they were served a meal by the dignitaries, in memory of our Lord's act of humility in washing the feet of his disciples. The 'Maundy' was observed in England by royalty, the nobility and by private individuals who on this day entertained the poor in their great houses.

This day was also known as 'Absolution Day' where the penitents, after confessing their sins to a priest, received from him a token of God's acceptance of their repentance by a rod being placed on their heads. On certain occasions this custom was taken somewhat far where the priest actually beat the hands of the penitents.

GOOD FRIDAY BED-MAKING

IN Tenby, Pembrokeshire, even up until the beginning of the nineteenth century old people walked barefoot to the parish church on Good Friday. It was in this part of 'little England beyond Wales' that the young people got together in Holy Week to 'make Christ's bed'. In order to do this large quantities of reeds were gathered from the river and these were woven into the shape of a man. This figure was then laid on a wooden cross and placed in a secluded part of a field.

EVERLASTING BREAD

IT was believed that buns baked on a Good Friday never went mouldy, and they were believed to possess healing properties. Even the bakers themselves kept some of their own hot cross buns for luck.

HOLY SATURDAY

ON the evening of the Saturday before Easter Sunday, the Paschal Candle was lit. This was done by striking steel on flint and the candle was taken in procession from outside the west door into the church to be blessed by the priest. Five grains of incense were placed in the candle to remind people of Christ's five sacred wounds. The term Paschal was given to the tall, thick piece of wood painted to represent a candle on top of which the real candle was placed. For some reason, lost in the ages, the wooden part was called by our English ancestors, the Judas of the Paschal.

EASTER OFFERING

AT Easter during the Middle Ages the churchwardens had to collect 'Peter's Pence', 'Rome Fardynges', 'Rome's scot' or 'Peter Fardynges', which was the contribution from each household to the Pope. It is doubtful whether more than 50 per cent of the amount collected ever found its way to

Rome. The wardens collected the money and paid it to the archdeacon at the time of his visitation.

Another such collection made by the churchwardens was called 'Wax-silver', or in some places called 'Candle-silver', 'Easter Money', or 'Paschal Money'. These payments were made in many parishes towards the annual expense of buying candles and oil for the lamps to burn in church.

A-MAYING BEFORE THE RED FLAG

MAY DAY in the seventeenth century was always kept as a holiday with much dancing and revelry. In his poem 'Corinna's going a-Maying', (1648) Herrick records the custom of placing boughs of May over each door:

> Each Porch, each doore, ere this,
> An Arke a Tabernacle is
> Made up of white-thorn neatly enterwove,
> As if here were those whose cooler shades of love.

Again he says:

> A deale of Youth, ere this, is come
> Back, and with White-thorn laden home.
> Some have dispatcht their Cakes and Creame,
> Before that we have left to dreame.

SHADES OF ST MICHAEL

ON the three days before the feast of the Ascension there was an ancient custom for people to process through the streets or country roads of the parish. These were days of Intercession and the processions were all important. The cross went at the head of the procession and on the first two days an image of a dragon with its tail was carried before

173

the procession and on the third day, without its tail, after the procession.

HOLY H$_2$O DAY

IN past generations, Ascension Day or 'Holy Thursday,' had a particular significance where water was concerned. Rain that was caught in a bowl on that day was said to be holy water coming straight from heaven. This water was preserved and used as a cure for weak or sore eyes. In Cowbridge, Glamorganshire, on Ascension Day, parties of children were provided with cups and sugar. Water was then drawn from the local holy well, the sugar added and then consumed by the children.

WELL DONE FLOWER ARRANGEMENTS

IN certain parishes in which natural springs exist, the wells, as they are called, are elaborately decorated with flowers. The origin of this custom was to offer thanks to God for the blessing of a good supply of water.

There is one such well in the parish of St Alkmund, Derby. The legend concerning this well is that, about the year 940, some monks carrying the remains of St Alkmund from the North for interment in Derby, to prevent their desecration by the invading Danes, made their last rest by this well before entering the town, and for years afterwards the water was supposed to possess marvellous curative powers.

In dressing the well at Whitsuntide a scriptural subject is invariably incorporated into the scheme of decoration.

DEVIL EXCLUSION

ON the eve of St John the Baptist sprigs of St John's wort or in lieu of it, the common Mugwort, were stuck over the doors. The intent was to cleanse the house of evil spirits. This custom seems to have been derived from the practice of the Druids who did the same with Vervaine, which still bears the Welsh name of Cas gan Cythrael, or the demon's aversion.

A THUMPING OCCASION

IN some districts of Yorkshire the Sunday following 28th June was called 'Thump Sunday', when people visited their friends and neighbours to eat spiced cake and cheese.

ST SWITHUN'S FARTHINGS

THERE was an old custom in the early days of bringing farthings to church on St Swithun's Day, 15th July, to present to the parish priest. The reason for this offering is lost in antiquity, but it is probable that the person giving the gift felt that his crop, especially if it were an apple crop, would be more plentiful if he placated the saint. St Swithun is said to be 'Christening the little apples if rain falls upon this day'.

I LIKEN HIS GRACE TO AN ACORNED HOG

IT was an old Sussex custom to ring the hogs before the festival of St Michael and All Angels and they were to remain so ringed until the following feast of St John the Baptist, under pain of forfeiting to the lord of the manor, 'for every hog, for every week, 3s. 4d.'.

HARVEST HOME

CORN dolls or corn babies were sometimes made out of the

last corn reaped. Corn was used to make the shape of a child and varied in size from 3ft to a minute 'neck'. These figures were made in the field then seized by a harvester who ran as hard as he could to the farmhouse through a gauntlet of his fellow harvesters trying to pour water on it. If it got wet then it was an omen that the harvest the following year would not be good. The doll was usually hung over the mantlepiece in the farmhouse until it was replaced the following year—rather like the Palm Cross.

It is important to remember that before the age of the machine the reaping of the ripe corn was done by sickle and scythe, one man reaping about three-quarters of an acre a day. Men, women and children would be in the field from dawn until well on into the night. No wonder they saw the power of God in the corn. It gave them food and became the symbol of the Resurrection—of death and new life.

> They took a plow and plowed him in,
> Laid clods upon his head,
> And they have taken a solemn oath
> John Barleycorn is dead.

> So there he lay for a full fortnight
> Till dew did on him fall;
> Then Barleycorn sprung up again
> And that surprised them all.

> There he remained till midsummer
> And looked both pale and wan,
> Then Barleycorn he got a beard,
> And so became a man.

Then they sent men with scythes so sharp
To cut him off at knee;
And then poor Johnny Barleycorn
They served him barbarously.

      Bell's 'Songs of the Peasantry of England'

SOUL BAKING

ON All Souls' Day, 2nd November, children used to go round the houses begging specially baked cakes, chanting:

Soul, soul, for a soul cake;
Pray, good mistress, for a soul cake,
One for Peter, two for Paul,
Three for them that made us all.

INDEX

187

189